Twayne's English Authors Series

Sylvia E. Bowman, *Editor*
INDIANA UNIVERSITY

Noel Coward

(TEAS) 73

Noel Coward

By MILTON LEVIN
Trenton State College

820840

TWAYNE PUBLISHERS
A DIVISION OF G. K. HALL & CO., BOSTON

To My Muses:
Mimi and Melissa

Contents

Preface

For more than half a century, Noel Coward has been standing down front, center stage, in the full brilliance of the spotlight, holding the audience entranced with his songs, his plays, his films, his stories, and above all, with himself. Few people can probably name more than two or three Coward titles without considerable strain on the memory, but who does not have a vivid image when the man is mentioned? Noel Coward's reputation as a writer and as a performer of great versatility, astonishing productiveness, and marvelous polish is unassailable.

It is difficult to deal with Coward strictly as an author because he is still so very much present as a performer. After seeing him in a play, or hearing him on a recording, or even just watching him being interviewed on a television program, can one ever again read his works without hearing an echo of that languorous voice with its ironic edge, or sensing, even more than seeing, that slightly curling lip and the cool eyes? Dramatic literature is notoriously difficult to discuss because the printed text can never fully be called the whole work, but in Coward's case this problem is greatly intensified because so many of his scripts were prepared with the author planning to perform one of the leading roles or at least direct the first production.

A great frustration to the critic anxious to shine is created by Coward's choice of genres and success with all of them. He has concentrated his energies on high farce, on smart high comedy, on domestic and patriotic melodrama, and on musical comedies and revues. Furthermore, he has usually been content to accept these forms very much in the shape in which the popular theater has developed them; and, when he has introduced his own variations and inventions, they have almost always tended to enhance the elegance and brilliance of the surface, rarely adding to the depths. Thus, beyond synopsis and quotation, the better the plays the more they resist critical discussion: they raise no questions; they provide few critical footholds. They simply ask to be praised for what they are, sparkling caprices.

Time and experience have helped Coward to sharpen his tools, but the finished works differ little in intent or in execution—no matter where they come in his career; and a chronological discussion, suggesting a line of evolution or hinting at a pattern of response to historical or biographical occasions, would be seriously misleading. (A few works were stimulated by specific circumstances, as will be explained in the course of this study; but they are by no means typical.) Also, Coward's practice of alternating his works—following a revue with a serious play, for example, or a farce with a sentimental operetta, and that with a collection of short stories, that with a film, etc.—makes a chronological approach inoperable. Each work would need to be discussed almost entirely in isolation.

To organize the discussion around a concern for Coward's themes would be even less helpful; for, few in number, they are presented with very little variation from item to item, and most important, are not so much a reflection of Coward's interest in morality or society but show instead the traditional interests of the genres: the course of true love in the operettas, the defense of sophisticated adultery in the comedies, the bittersweet rhythms of domestic life in the dramas, and the staunch, stiff-upper-lip endurance of the patriotic plays. Such development and variation as can profitably be examined in Coward's work are best presented, therefore, by grouping the works according to type, by outlining the pattern of each type as Coward has normally seen it, and then by discussing the individual examples. Aside from the opening biography and the concluding chapter, this has been the pattern for this book.

MILTON LEVIN

Trenton State College

Acknowledgments

Permissions to quote from the following works are gratefully acknowledged.

From "Ashes of Roses" from *Star Quality* by Noel Coward. Copyright 1951 by Noel Coward. Reprinted by permission of Doubleday & Company, Inc.

From *Bitter-Sweet* by Noel Coward. Copyright 1929 by Noel Coward. Reprinted by permission of Doubleday & Company, Inc.

From *Blithe Spirit* by Noel Coward. Copyright 1941 by Noel Coward. Reprinted by permission of Doubleday & Company, Inc.

From *Cavalcade* by Noel Coward. Copyright 1931, 1932 by Noel Coward. Reprinted by permission of Doubleday & Company, Inc.

From *Design for Living* by Noel Coward. Copyright 1933 by Noel Coward. Reprinted by permission of Doubleday & Company, Inc.

From *Hay Fever* by Noel Coward. Copyright 1925 by Noel Coward. Reprinted by permission of Doubleday & Company, Inc.

From "If You Could Only Come With Me." Copyright 1921 by Chappell & Company, Ltd. Copyright renewed and assigned to Harms, Inc. Used by permission.

From "Introduction" copyright 1933 by Noel Coward. From *Play Parade* Volume I, by Noel Coward. Reprinted by permission of Doubleday & Company, Inc.

From "Introduction" copyright 1950 by Noel Coward. From *Play Parade* Volume II. Reprinted by permission of Doubleday & Company, Inc.

From "Lie in the Dark and Listen." Copyright 1943 by Noel Coward. Used by permission of Curtis Brown Ltd.

From "Love of My Dreams" ("Mirabelle Waltz"). Copyright 1931 by Chappell & Co., Ltd. Copyright renewed. Used by permission of Chappell & Co., Inc.

Chronology

Noel Coward's life has been so thoroughly and almost exclusively devoted to writing and performing that a list of all his activities—writing, acting, directing, travelling—would be voluminous. The following offers only a sketch of his biography as a whole, combining the few obviously significant dates with a number chosen as representative rather than decisive. It must be borne in mind that since 1911 not a year has passed without the production of at least one new Coward play, the publication of some non-dramatic writing, or at least one appearance by him in a play, a film or a solo program; and most years have witnessed a wide assortment of activities.

1899   Noel Coward born, December 16, at Teddington, Middlesex, to Arthur Sabin and Violet Veitch Coward. The Cowards' first child, Russell, had died at the age of six, a year and a half before Noel's birth. Their only other child, Eric, was born in 1905.

1907   July 23; first public appearance, at end-of-term concert by the pupils of St. Margaret's, Sutton.

1911   January 27; professional debut as Prince Mussel in *The Goldfish.*

1912   February 2; directed, for a special matinee, a one-act play, *The Daisy Chain,* by Dot Temple, eleven years old, appearing with him in *Where the Rainbow Ends.*

1918   Brief period of army service, spent mostly in hospitals. Wrote *The Rat Trap,* the earliest Coward play available in print; first produced in 1926.

1919   August; played Ralph in *The Knight of the Burning Pestle,* by Beaumont and Fletcher, at Birmingham Repertory Theatre.

1919   Sold *The Last Trick* to Al Woods for $2,000; Woods bought it to have it rewritten by a more experienced playwright, but it was never produced.

1920   May 3; *I'll Leave It to You* produced in Manchester, Coward playing Bobbie Dermott. July 21; *I'll Leave It to You* first produced in London, Coward repeating the same role. First production of a Coward play.

1921   First trip to America; stayed some months in New York, made many friends, sold some parodies and short stories, but failed to interest anyone in his plays.

1922   September 25; *The Young Idea* produced in Bristol, Coward playing Sholto Brent; production in London, February 1, 1923. Publication of *A Withered Nosegay*, collection of burlesque biographies; published the same year in America as *Terribly Intimate Portraits*.

1923   September 4; appeared in *London Calling!*, a revue of which he was the chief author.

1924   November 25; *The Vortex* produced in Hampstead, Coward playing the leading role of Nicky Lancaster; production transferred to London, December 16. This production brought fame to Coward both as playwright and as actor.

1926   September; appeared as Lewis Dodd in *The Constant Nymph*, by Margaret Kennedy and Basil Dean, one of the few times after 1925 when Coward appeared in a work by another author.

1928   January; appeared as Clark Storey in *The Second Man*, by S. N. Behrman.

1929   July 2; first production of *Bitter-Sweet*, Coward's first "operette." November, through spring of 1930; second of many trips to the Pacific and the Orient. On this trip, he wrote *Private Lives* and *Post-Mortem*.

1931   October 13; opening of *Cavalcade* at the Theatre Royal, Drury Lane, London; Coward's most spectacular production and one of his most famous.

1934   First major film appearance, in *The Scoundrel*, written and directed by Ben Hecht and Charles McArthur.

1937   Publication of *Present Indicative*, first volume of autobiography.

1939   September, to April 1940; held post in Enemy Propaganda Office, Paris. Publication of *To Step Aside*, first collection of short stories.

1941 July 2; opening of *Blithe Spirit*, to run for 1,997 performances, the English record for a straight play, broken on September 13, 1957, by the 1,998th performance of Agatha Christie's *The Mousetrap*. July; began work on script for *In Which We Serve*, only Coward film not adapted from a play. *In Which We Serve* was produced by Noel Coward and directed by Noel Coward and David Lean; the major role of Captain "D" was performed by Coward. The film was first shown in London on September 27, 1942.

1943 Summer; visiting and entertaining in army camps, hospitals, in the Middle East.

1944 January through July; entertaining in army camps, hospitals, etc. in South Africa, Ceylon, India and Australia.

1951 October; beginning, at Café de Paris, London, of highly successful career as a cabaret performer.

1953 May; appeared as King Magnus in *The Apple Cart* by Bernard Shaw.

1955 October 22; appeared with Mary Martin in *Together with Music*, a ninety-minute television production written by and directed by Noel Coward.

1956 Coward announced that he had given up residence in England and planned to spend his time chiefly in Jamaica.

1960 Publication of *Pomp and Circumstance*, a comic novel.

1964 November; revival of *Hay Fever* by English National Theatre, London.

1966 April; appeared in the leading roles of all three plays included in *Suite in Three Keys*.

CHAPTER 1

Biography

NOEL COWARD was not born backstage at a music hall, nor was his mother rushed to the maternity hospital from a table at the Café de Paris. How appropriate it would be if his story "Aunt Tittie," about a young boy's introduction to all the glamor and squalor of European cabaret life, were autobiographical. But life in Coward's case was less lavish in poetic appropriateness, for he was born in Teddington, Middlesex, a middle-class suburb of London, on December 16, 1899. The Coward family, including a large number of aunts and uncles, was "enormous, active, and fiercely musical";[1] but these factors were not unusual for the time, and there were no obvious omens.

The fullest picture of Coward's early years is in his first volume of autobiography, *Present Indicative;* and there is little reason to quarrel with his statement that "I don't believe that my own childhood, until I went on the stage at the age of ten, was very different from that of any other little boy of the middle-classes, except that certain embryonic talents may have made me more precocious than the average." [2] Only hindsight can confer much significance on his success as an entertainer at school programs or in children's competitions at seaside "concert parties." Patrick Braybrooke, Coward's first biographer,[3] devotes considerable space to Coward's difficulties in school, caused by his drawing stage settings and writing bits of dialogue; but Mr. Braybrooke does not give the source of his information (one suspects him of giving his imagination free rein in order to support his labeling of the infant Noel Coward as a "baby of genius"); and in any case these activities are common enough. Even Coward's professional debut had its familiar elements: poverty, and an ambitious, persistent mother.

Shortly after Coward's birth, his father took a job with a new piano firm. By 1908, a number of moves had brought the family to the edge of poverty; for Payne's pianos were unpopular. For a while, paying guests helped. Then the London apartment was let while the Cowards lived frugally in a tiny country cottage, but money problems persisted. As for Noel, an audition for the school and choir of the Chapel Royal proved unsuccessful; but, since he continued to shine in amateur concerts and theatricals, his mother decided that dancing lessons might prove a good investment. So they did, after Mrs. Coward discovered an advertisement for "a talented boy of attractive appearance" to appear in an all-children, fairy play: *The Goldfish*. The audition was successful, and Coward was launched on a professional career as Prince Mussel.

The Goldfish opened in London on January 27, 1911; and, from that time on, Coward's time "was divided between school and stage engagements of an ever-increasing importance" and variety. None of the roles was a leading one; many consisted of only a few lines. However, Coward found the work immediately congenial and the experience and training provided can hardly be overestimated. For the first few years, he appeared mostly in fantasies with casts consisting entirely or mainly of children (for example, he appeared in three different companies playing *Peter Pan* between December, 1913, and January, 1915). He experienced the thrill of applause and learned to project personal charm and vitality beyond the footlights in order to attract even more adulation. The exaltation that came from applause and praise was also a stimulus that started Coward writing. Most of what he wrote, whether poems, short stories, songs, plays, skits or novels, was first aimed at his contemporaries, other adolescents working in the theater and writing.

Stoj [Esme Wynne] was determined to be a writer, an ambition that filled me with competitive fervor. She wrote poems. Reams and reams of them, love songs, sonnets, and vilanelles. . . . Not to be outdone in artistic endeavour, I set many of the poems to music, sometimes, owing to the exigencies of my inspiration, changing her original scansion with disastrous results. . . . Very soon I began to write short stories, beastly little whimsies, . . . about Pan, and fauns and cloven hooves. We read a lot of Oscar Wilde and Omar Khayyam and Laurence Hope.[4]

Soon he began creating theatrical material in which he could appear.

Sometimes there were long periods when Coward was out of work, and one period when he was confined to his bed with "a tubercular gland in [his] chest"; but the first important interruption of the accelerating rhythm of success was Coward's "brief and inglorious" stay in the British Army. Too young for the army when the war began, Coward was finally called in 1918, at a time when "the spirit of sacrifice, the conviction of speedy victory, and even the sense of national pride had faded in the minds of most people in a cheerless resignation." [5] Because of his "T.B. tendency," he was at first assigned to a Labour Corps; but he succeeded in having himself reassigned to the Artists' Rifles. Almost at once, however, Coward was beset by headaches, attacks of fainting, and general "neuresthenia." After a number of months, spent mostly in hospitals, Coward was discharged.

For most of the next two years he had to depend on a few small parts and on the sales of stories to magazines. He also bolstered his income with fees from a music publishing firm with which he signed a three-year contract to provide song lyrics; he was conscientiously paid the contracted fee although apparently he did not submit much material and very little of what he did submit was used. He was, however, writing a good deal—short stories, a novel, and plays—and a meeting with Gilbert Miller, the successful American producer, proved eventful. Miller thought that Coward's melodrama, *The Last Trick*, was promising and encouraged him to go on writing. In time, Al Woods, through Miller, paid Coward for a year's option on the play; but it was never produced or published. Then Miller suggested the idea for *I'll Leave it to You*, which opened in Manchester in May, 1920, and in London two months later. From this point on, Coward's biography is primarily the history of his work.

I   Behind the Scenes

If the preceding sketch is scanty, it is not for lack of materials; not only has Coward been one of the most conspicuous figures in this age of publicity, but he has had a hand in the shaping of modern patterns of celebrity and notoriety. During the excitement following the opening of *The Vortex*, he released "a photograph of himself in bed, wearing a Chinese dressing-gown in a scarlet bedroom decorated with nudes, his expression being one of advanced degeneracy." [6] Since then he has conscientiously at-

tempted to correct the impression of dalliance this picture and his
early plays created, and certainly the very volume of his work is a
corrective; however, he has remained solidly identified with the
life of monied and conspicuous idleness. Whether the chic group
has been called "café society" or the "jet set," Coward and his
model insouciance have been somewhere in the picture. Of
course, his new plays, films, performances, plans, and travels have
always been considered news and have been amply chronicled.

In addition to this public information, Coward has provided a
detailed account of the period preceding his early success in *Present Indicative*, while *Future Indicative, Middle-East Diary*, and
many prefaces and interviews have provided space for him to
present his more serious, hard-working side. Yet, even when the
important information is separated from the gossip, it seems irrelevant insofar as being a contribution to an understanding of his
work. Except for a brief period during 1939–1940 when he
worked for the British Secret Service in Paris, Coward's life has
been virtually inseparable from the world of entertainment.

Coward has travelled a good deal during most of his life; but,
aside from providing local color for a few of the plays and some
fiction, the travel has contributed little to his work; what it has
contributed and in what ways Coward's experiences in both world
wars have affected his work are more fittingly discussed in connection with the works themselves. He has indicated in some
places that he has suffered from time to time from what appeared
to be mild nervous breakdowns or from something comparable to
the "neuresthenia" he suffered in the army, but his writing is almost entirely free of related materials, nor can one trace in the
works changing patterns of value or a deepening understanding
of behavior which is in any way attributable to personal crisis.

Where Coward grows in awareness and psychological complexity, the reasons lie mainly with his growing competence as a
writer—with practice, observation, age, and experience, and even
more with his sensitivity to the abilities of his actors, including
himself, and to changing theater tastes. His domestic life has consisted mostly of providing comfortable, spacious homes for his
parents while they were alive, and for himself since. He has not
married, and there is no evidence in his writing or elsewhere of
any serious emotional attachment other than to his mother. If reticence and a taste for camouflage have concealed further evidence

on this subject, it is doubtful whether revealing it would make much difference. Coward's plays and stories fall so clearly within certain stylized patterns that parallels with his own life would not be illuminating even if established. In short, Coward's work is independent of his personal life regardless of how much the aura of his fame suggests a glamorous, sophisticated life of which the plays and stories are at best only a few crumbs from the banquet table.

II *The Popular Theater*

Limiting our view to Coward purely as a writer presents some difficulties because this is the one area where there are gaps in the record. Although he has written fully about many of his experiences, the people he has met and worked with, and the places he has been, and although he has shown a willingness, in prefaces and especially in introductions, to comment on technical difficulties and to judge his own works, Coward has provided little information about what he has read, what plays or playwrights he admires, and what models he took for his early work. What he did come to know thoroughly was the popular theater of the 1910's and 1920's, and it is for this theater that all of his work has, in effect, been written. It is significant that Coward ends his account of his early years with the production of *Cavalcade*, virtually a Valentine to Coward's early love and a proof that he had mastered the full range of popular theater as it appeared to him from his first visit on his fifth birthday.

Literary historians tend to concentrate on masterworks and on innovations. Since in the history of modern drama the two tend to be virtually synonymous, it is easy to derive the impression that the line stretching from Ibsen and Strindberg to Williams and Ionesco is not only the most important but practically the only one. The record of any recent New York or London season will demonstrate how inaccurate this inference is, for most productions are of works that make little pretense of challenging the moral or esthetic ideas of the audience. Ibsen's statement in *An Enemy of the People* that the compact majority is always a generation behind the true thinkers may well be, when applied to the theater, one of the greatest understatements of all time.

In the early decades of this century, the disparity was even greater between the plays that now bulk so large in histories and

anthologies and those that actually dominated the stage. The in-
roads made by the avant-garde were very small, and the cinema
(silent until the late 1920's) had not yet seriously reduced the size
of the play-going public. In the years before, during and for some
time following World War I, an enormous number of productions
appeared each year. The theater of light entertainment was flourishing; the long run record of 2,238 performances was set by *Chu
Chin Chow* by the time it closed in July, 1921, a record not disturbed for forty years.

Nor was a possible long run for a play necessary to justify producing it. The cost of production was small enough and the audience large enough to allow for a number of inexpensive, transient
presentations in addition to the more elaborate ones. During 1927,
for example, *Theatre World* never reviewed fewer than five new
London productions each month, winter or summer, and some
months as many as fifteen (this datum does not include the
Christmas pantomimes and other special events). And a good
many lasted long enough to be rated as at least nominal successes.
Coward's first play to reach London, *I'll Leave it to You,* had
thirty-seven performances, hardly a disaster; his second, *The
Young Idea,* had sixty and could reasonably be counted a success.

Few of the productions during those years made any pretension
to being anything but entertainment in the simplest sense of that
word: operettas, spectacles, pantomimes, frivolous comedies, melodramas, and "strong" plays (melodramas with an added fillip
created by the introduction of squalid situations and/or the illusion of moral dilemmas involving alcoholics, prostitutes, and the
like). In short, the theater then was not too unlike the popular
theater of today. There was, however, one important distinction: it
was in those early decades more definitely popular than it is today, attracting a large audience that went to the theater frequently and unselfconsciously, unashamedly asking to be amused,
touched, or thrilled rather than scolded, harrowed, or uplifted—
the audience, in fact, that now goes exclusively to musicals and
the very lightest of comedies, if it goes to the theater at all.

As Prince Mussel in *The Goldfish,* Noel Coward entered this
world; and he has never wavered in his intention to win and retain success in that milieu. Praise from the more serious, more
literary critics was never amiss; but this audience was not the one
in whom Coward was ever greatly interested. His versatility in

itself is evidence of how thoroughly he has always belonged to the popular theater, for not only is it a versatility encompassing all the modes of popular entertainment, but it virtually demands cheers for itself, like the skill of the tightrope walker who astonishes by riding a bicycle on the tightrope, then adds juggling to his act, and finally, after letting his trousers slip down to reveal a pair of long red drawers, exits amid a roar of laughter coupled with a thunder of applause.

When the production of *The Vortex,* an excellent example of a "strong" play, made Coward, aged twenty-four, a name to reckon with, he had already written both the words and music for a revue, *London Calling;* two other "strong" plays, *The Rat Trap* and *Sirocco;* a Ruritanian melodrama, *The Queen Was in the Parlour;* and six comedies, two of which had already been produced. Over the years, his work has remained astonishingly varied; but, through it all, he has apparently never forgotten the thrill of his first role when, as Prince Mussel, he sang a song in the last act and "was invariably encored, sometimes twice." *Post Mortem,* the one play in which Coward tried to dramatize some of his deepest convictions and to use some slightly expressionistic techniques "was not actually written for the theatre," he says. This is true, if by *theatre* Coward means entertainment for the mass audience.

He recently defined his audience, "the great public," and his attitude toward it:

I believe that the great public by which I've lived all these years should not be despised or patronized or forced to accept esoteric ideas in the theater in the name of culture or social problems or what not. I'm sick of the assumption that plays are "important" only if they deal with some extremely urgent current problem.

Problems? We live with them all day, every day, all our lives. Do we have to have them in the theater every night, too? I was brought up in the belief that the theater is primarily a place of entertainment.

The audience wants to laugh or cry or be amused. Swift entertainment—not strange allegories.[7]

The pre-war theater was not only dedicated to entertainment; it was also a place in which the actor-manager was still king. The actor-manager was the fullest flowering of the "star" in a theater where economics had not yet achieved control. Today, production is the result of a combination of forces: the author, the actors, the director, the producer, and the financial backers. The actor-manager, however, had the last word on everything; because of his popularity, he could either employ his own funds or draw on uncritical supporters; because the director as we know him today was virtually unknown, the actor-manager handled all his functions, as he organized the whole production to set off his own performance. Because he was, and intended to remain, the center of attraction, he chose plays that suited his frequently limited talents, he used malleable authors to supply him with "vehicles," or he freely adapted and rewrote plays to suit his purposes. A summary of the many weaknesses and few virtues of the system can be found in Shaw's essay on Beerbohm Tree, which concludes,

But the heart of the matter . . . is that the cure of the disease of actor-managership (every author must take that pathological view of it) is actor-author-managership: the cure of Moliere, who acted his plays as well as wrote them, and managed his theatre into the bargain. And yet he lasted fifty-one years. . . . Tree should have written his own plays. . . . He would have taken a parental pride in other parts beside his own. He would have come to care for a play as a play, and to understand that it has powers over the audience even when it is read by people sitting around a table or performed by wooden marionettes. . . . And it would have given him what he was always craving from authors, and in the nature of the case could never get from them: a perfect projection of the great Tree personality.[8]

In many ways, Coward satisfies Shaw's prescription remarkably well, except in regard to managing a theater. He has appeared almost exclusively in work of his own authorship, and he has directed almost all his works, whether he appeared in them or not. Most important of all, as the body of this study shows, Shaw's idea about "parental pride in other parts beside his own" is one of the keys to Coward's best work.

Noel Coward's own early idol among actor-managers was Charles Hawtrey, who specialized in drawing-room comedy. Coward's second professional role was that of a page boy in Hawtrey's production of *The Great Name*, by James Clarence Harvey, and he appeared in Hawtrey's company off and on for a number of years. Hawtrey taught him a good deal, including the dangers of overacting, of wanting always to be the center of attraction. The largest role Coward ever played with the Hawtrey company was in *The Saving Grace*, written by Haddon Chambers, who, in the early decades of this century, was highly regarded as a writer of wit. Today his plays seem stilted and sentimental, but he does occasionally surprise with a line or speech that has the rhythm and verve of high comedy. In his *Passers-by* (1911), for example, Waverton, the young man about town, discovers his butler entertaining a cabman in the living-room: "In taking my tobacco and whisky, you exceed your duty, Pine. . . . In using my room to entertain your friend you permitted yourself a gross liberty. . . . And in throwing away, half-smoked, one of my best cigars, you committed a crime." [9]

A writer like Chambers, fashionably witty and mildly satirical, can tell us more about Coward's literary antecedents than can the far-better known and respected writers of the period, like Shaw and Maugham. Coward sent the script for *The Young Idea* to Shaw and was delighted to receive it back "scribbled all over with alterations and suggestions," along with a long letter that said in effect that he "showed every indication of becoming a good playwright," providing that he never again in his life "read another word that he, Shaw, had written." Coward says that he took this advice "only half-heartedly"; but, consciously or not, his work shows little indebtedness to Shaw. Insofar as Shaw played a major role in bringing more natural dialogue onto the stage and an even more important role in challenging moral conventions, Coward, along with all modern playwrights, owes Shaw an immense debt. And no doubt Shaw's wit could hardly go unnoticed by a young playwright eager to succeed. However, even though Coward modelled his central characters in *The Young Idea* on the twins in Shaw's *You Never Can Tell*, the heart of Shaw's work—the combat of ideas—is alien to Coward's writing. His occasional attacks on hypocrisy and stuffy conventionality have far more in common with Chambers than with Shaw.

Coward's relationship with Maugham seems at first considerably more important. His admiration for the older man is evident in many ways: Coward asked Maugham to write an introduction for one of the earliest publications of his plays, and Maugham responded with a very flattering one. In at least three of Coward's plays, *Point Valaine, South Sea Bubble*, and *A Song at Twilight*, Maugham quite clearly served as a model for the novelist characters, and the first play is dedicated to him. In *Relative Values* there is a highly flattering reference to Maugham as a playwright, one of the very few references to any author in Coward's works.

Yet the amount of direct influence seems to be small. Echoes of Maugham can be heard in a few plays, particularly *Point Valaine* and *Fumed Oak;* many of Coward's short stories are rather similar to Maugham's; and both men share an attitude of worldly disillusion and cynicism. It may be that Coward learned some things from Maugham's plays: the importance of careful preparation, the art of writing love scenes between reticent people (consider the scenes between Elizabeth and Teddy in *The Circle*), and the techniques needed to keep apparently irrelevant and spontaneous dialogue moving. However, this is more a matter of affinity between the two men and a response to strong currents in the theater of the time than a matter of direct influence. Maugham's interest in moral and social questions, so much less dynamic and revolutionary than Shaw's but always definitely present, finds hardly any echo in Coward's work. In a few of his very earliest plays—*The Rat Trap, Easy Virtue, Sirocco,* even *The Vortex*—something like Maugham's seriousness can be observed; but Coward soon discovered that this was not his territory.

Coward was a child of the popular theater. His earliest play available today, *The Rat Trap,* written when he was eighteen, differs hardly at all in type from any number of plays available in London around 1920, nor does it differ much from the work that was to occupy him for the next half century. Its gaucherie reflects its author's age and inexperience, but its point of view and basic style are the same as those in his most recent work. Where *The Rat Trap* differs from, say, Chambers' *The Tyranny of Tears* is in its far greater moral relativism and in the general air of smartness. In this respect Coward shows himself the child not only of the popular theater but of the 1920's as a whole.

III *Fashionable Disillusion*

The new keyword was Disillusion—not the Byronic melancholy and the Sorrows of Werther which had been in fashion after the Napoleonic Wars, but a hard, cynical, gay disillusion. It needed a poet for its expression, and there was T. S. Eliot waiting. His "Love-Song of J. Alfred Prufrock" and "Preludes" struck just the right note. . . . His "Waste Land" . . . appeared in the *Criterion* in 1922. . . .[10]

Coward was the dramatist of disillusion, as Eliot was its tragic poet, Aldous Huxley its novelist, and James Joyce its prose epic-writer. They all had in common a sense of the unreality of time. The main theme of the revues that Coward wrote for C. B. Cochran was that one now knew a little too much for happiness; and that this was a "period" period, without a style for its own any longer, but with full liberty to borrow from any wardrobe of the past. His songs "World-Weary" and "Dance, Dance, Dance Little Lady" were felt to reflect the mood of his time.[11]

This disillusionment in the plays of Coward is one side of the coin; and, if it were the only one, Coward would be a glum figure indeed. But disillusion was also a release and a source of social revolution. "We have grown big enough to understand," said Coward in 1927, "that life, *real* life, must be submitted to the closest scrutiny if we are to learn how to deal with it." [12] Some results of that scrutiny were the change in manners and in values which have come to be associated with the 1920's: greater freedom for women; freedom from long hair and corsets, as well as greater economic freedom; the right to vote and to enter the professions; the right to go dancing without a chaperone; the chance to practice, or at least talk about, "companionate marriage" and birth control; and greater freedom of language and behavior for all, nicely spiced by opposing and shocking the prudish Old Guard. Disillusion may have been at the heart of the mood of the 1920's, but the surface showed more of abandon and gaiety. Coward may have written a song entitled "World-Weary" and helped make disenchantment and world-weariness signs of sophistication, but there was nothing depressing about it all.

It was the time of the Bright Young Things and of bright young men who could make their fortunes by capturing and exemplifying the prevailing mood. Two of Coward's friends of this period provide an observation point. Like Coward, Ivor Novello and Michael Arlen came from unpromising backgrounds and achieved celebrity at an early age. Novello, six years older than Coward, became famous early during World War I with his song "Keep the Home Fires Burning." He appeared in films, and wrote, directed, and starred in a series of most successful plays and operettas. For the most part his plays and musicals are sentimental.

Novello was destined to become the very prototype of the matinee idol, mourned by great crowds of middle-aged women when he died in 1952. In 1916, when Coward met him, Novello was already becoming well-known: "I envied thoroughly everything about him. His looks, his personality, his assured position, his dinner clothes, his bedroom and bath, and above all, the supper party. . . . I just felt suddenly conscious of the way I had to go before I could break into the magic atmosphere in which he moved and breathed with such nonchalance." [13]

The same attitudes, particularly the pose of nonchalance, are present in a passage about Michael Arlen (four years older than Coward): "Michael Arlen was also just beginning to blossom about this time [1919]. We used to wave languidly to each other across dance floors, shedding our worldliness later, in obscure corners. He was very dapper, and his Hawes and Curtis backless waistcoats aroused envy in me, which I soon placated, by ordering some for myself, but his exquisite pearl and platinum watch chain was beyond competition, and all I could do was to admire it bravely, and hope, in my heart, that perhaps it was just a little bit ostentatious." [14]

Arlen's success was slated to be more limited than Novello's and Coward's, but in the 1920's Arlen was as successful as anyone could wish: "Soon he became not only a popular writer but a vogue, with his regular table at the Embassy Club each night, and a familiar long yellow Rolls-Royce waiting outside. Years later he confessed that he was a 'flash in the pan' in the twenties, but that by the grace of God there had been gold dust in the pan. . . . By 1939 he had made enough money, at a time when income tax was not excessively high, to retire." [15] His novel, *The Green Hat*, with its world-weary heroine, was the height of sophistication; Iris March was languid, too, and her clothes and cars (she, too, had a yellow Rolls) were "beyond competition" and a "little bit ostentatious." Many of Coward's heroines, Amanda Prynne in *Private Lives* for one, are Iris March's sisters.

In contrast to what Cyril Connolly has discovered to be the basic formula for the 1920's novel, "the bright young man and the dirty deal," Coward, Novello, and Arlen are three bright young men who figuratively broke the bank at Monte Carlo. In contrast to the post-World War II pattern of "angry young men" who are resolutely opposed to the Establishment, these three aimed at acceptance by the Establishment. They were rebels, but not revolutionaries; as men they embodied with chic the moral iconoclasm, the unconcern about politics and philosophical abstractions, the quest for gaiety and its corollary world-weariness, the unremittant thumbing of the nose at conventionality that were so characteristic of the well-to-do and well-educated of the decade before the Depression. Theirs was no anguished protest from below, only a dashing irreverence shared by the Very Best People. If Robert Graves groups Coward with Aldous Huxley, T. S. Eliot, and James Joyce as a spokesman for disillusion and if Frank Swinnerton groups him with Aldous Huxley, Richard Aldington, and Wyndham Lewis as a post-war pessimist, it is because no other playwright seemed to echo the fashionable accents of despair, the theater being as usual much slower to reflect intellectual change than poetry or the novel. However, time has shown that it was the accent which Coward captured—and hardly any of the substance.

Coward, unlike Novello, Arlen and a host of other chic writers of the 1920's, has remained both readable and actable without basically changing either his methods or his point of view. On the one hand, he is still the *enfant terrible* of 1924; on the other, he is still undated: "It is odd to find that young people, fresh to the theatre and ready to smile tolerantly at the odd stuff written in the dark ages before the war, usually treat Noel Coward as one of themselves. The name seems still to have a ring of youth. When Coward is in his sixties he will stay, in some queer fashion, as a symbol of youthful defiance, tapping out that defiance in the same witty Morse." [16] Perhaps the chapters to follow will explain why Coward has retained such popularity.

CHAPTER 2

Words and Music

TO begin a discussion of Noel Coward's work with his contribution to the musical theater is appropriate since that is
where his own earliest work appeared. By the time he was nine-
teen, he had "written quite a lot, in spare moments, . . . : plays
singly and in collaboration with Stoj [Esmé Wynne]. Short stories, verses and one meretricious full-length novel [*Cherry Pan*,
unpublished]. [He] had also composed a good many songs, and
written lyrics for some tunes of Max Darewski's and Doris
Joel's." [1] Of this material, the oldest surviving work is a song,
"Forbidden Fruit," written in 1915 but not publicly performed,
apparently, until it appeared in 1924 under the title "It's the
Peach" in *Yoicks!*, a revue. Before that, however, a song, "Peter
Pan," lyrics by Coward and music by Doris Joel, had appeared in
Tails Up! (1918); and *The Co-Optimists*, "A Pierrotic Entertain-
ment" that was presented with program variations for five sea-
sons, 1921–1926, used some Noel Coward items.

London Calling!, opening in September, 1923, truly introduced
Coward to the London musical theater, and in a revue which was
about three-quarters his work. It is tempting to over-emphasize
the significance of this now. At the time, however, revues were
one of the most common types of production, often consisting of
uncoordinated scraps and "acts." The exceptions to the type de-
rived from the taste and control exercised by the impresarios. The
two most important were André Charlot and C. B. Cochrane,
whose names were far more significant than those of the writers
and, in many cases, of the individual performers (the *Ziegfield
Follies* and *George White Scandals* in America were similar in this
respect). *London Calling!* was greeted and treated as a Charlot
revue, and it was not until Cochrane produced *This Year of
Grace!* in 1928, a revue entirely written and composed by Coward

by this time one of the best-known people in the London theater that the producer gave way to the writer in importance.

London Calling! played for 316 performances; and memories of Coward's skits, music, lyrics and performance added a distinct fillip to the opening of *The Vortex* in November, 1924. From that time on, Noel Coward, as composer, as playwright, as actor, as director, and frequently as a combination of two or more, has rarely been missing from the London and New York theaters. He has been responsible for thirteen musical productions, six of them revues, aside from contributions to revues mostly written by others. *The Girl Who Came to Dinner* (1963) is something of a departure since he provided only the songs.

I Victorian-Edwardian Music

A full discussion of the music is outside the scope of this book; nonetheless, a brief comment can be attempted, with the help of the composer himself:

I was born into a generation that still took light music seriously. The lyrics and melodies of Gilbert and Sullivan were hummed and strummed into my consciousness at an early age. . . . By the time I was four years old "Take a Pair of Sparkling Eyes," "Tit Willow," "We're Very Wide Awake, the Moon and I" and "I have a Song to Sing-O" had been fairly inculcated into my bloodstream.

The whole Edwardian era was saturated with operetta and musical comedy: in addition to popular foreign importations by Franz Lehar, Leo Fall, André Messager, etc., our own native composers were writing musical scores of a quality that has never been equalled in this country since the 1914–18 war. Lionel Monckton, Paul Rubens, Ivan Caryll and Leslie Stuart were flourishing. "The Quaker Girl," "Our Miss Gibbs," "Miss Hook to Holland," "Florodora," "The Arcadians" and "The Country Girl," to name only a few, were all fine musical achievements. . . .[2]

Coward is by no means exaggerating his admiration for Victorian and Edwardian music. *Bitter-Sweet,* probably his most successful and popular operette (Coward's preferred spelling), is set mostly in London and Vienna in the last quarter of the nineteenth century; its two most popular songs, "I'll See You Again" and "Zigeuner," are waltzes. *Operette* takes place in 1902 and concerns a theatrical group presenting "The Model Maid," a very gentle parody of the "Quaker Girl" type of operetta. The date in the title of *Pacific 1860* indicates its kinship with the others; and, although the action takes place on a Pacific island, the main characters are an English plantation owner's family and an opera singer who has come to the island to rest. The exotic setting is far less important than the Victorian costumes and attitudes. *Conversation Piece* is set in Brighton in 1811, but the score certainly owes more to Gilbert and Sullivan than to any Regency composer. In 1953, Coward adapted *Lady Windermere's Fan* as a musical, calling it *After the Ball;* and *The Girl Who Came to Dinner* takes place during the coronation of Edward VII. Only *The Ace of Clubs* and *Sail Away,* of the musical plays, are contemporary in setting and musical idiom.

Nor is the Victorian-Edwardian influence limited to these operettes. In *Cavalcade,* Coward used many older popular songs to date and set the mood for individual scenes; and he also composed three songs for the fragment of "Mirabelle," the musical play his heroine is attending in 1900 when the relief of Mafeking is announced. *In Tonight at 8:30,* "Family Album" is "A Victorian Comedy with Music." Finally, for *Private Lives,* Coward composed a waltz, "Someday I'll Find You," which has remained one of his most popular compositions; despite the brittle modern sophistication of the play as a whole, this song is as much in the Lehar idiom as is anything in *Bitter-Sweet.*

II   Negro-Jewish Rhythms

Coward's indebtedness to the Victorians and Edwardians, however, is only part of the picture. If much of his music, as well as the accompanying lyrics, shows both the influence of and a nostalgia for the music he heard in his childhood, the rest—primarily that of the revues—reflects what he has called the "vital Negro-Jewish rhythms from the New World." If the waltz is the typical musical form in most of the operettes and musical plays, the fox-trot and the blues are most typical of the revues. Nonetheless, excepting the comic songs, the Coward music which has been most popular has been that with a strong Victorian-Edwardian flavor, particularly the waltzes: "I'll See You Again," "Zigeuner," "Some Day I'll Find You," and "I'll Follow My Secret Heart."

When Coward evaluates his own music, he is proudest of those works which are most like those of the pre-war "generation that still took light music seriously":

> I have . . . composed many successful songs and three integrated scores of which I am genuinely proud. These are "Bitter Sweet," "Conversation Piece," and "Pacific 1860." "This Year of Grace" and "Words and Music," although revues, were also well-constructed musically. "Operette" was sadly meagre. . . . "Bitter Sweet," the most flamboyantly successful of all my musical shows, had a full and varied score. . . . "Conversation Piece" was less full and varied but had considerable quality. . . . "Pacific 1860" was, musically, my best work to date. It was carefully balanced and well constructed. . . .[3]

The three songs from *Pacific 1860* that Coward chose for *The Noel Coward Song Book* are "His Excellency Regrets" (a patter song) and "Bright was the Day" and "This is a Changing World," (both waltzes).

III *Problems of Love*

The subject matter of the musical plays is traditional: the vicissitudes of true love. Some end sadly—in *Bitter-Sweet,* Carl Linden is killed in a duel; in *Operette,* Roxanne nobly renounces her aristocratic lover so that his army career will not be ruined by marriage with an actress. These endings are no innovation; Victor Herbert's *Sweethearts,* with its pathetic ending, dates from 1913. On the whole, however, true love triumphs over the obstacles set in its way—a statement that is just as true of *Bitter-Sweet* and *Operette;* for Sarah Linden's life is still a graceful memorial to her love for Carl, and Roxanne's renunciation is a mark of truly unselfish love. Such is the world of the musical play and there is little mark of Coward's world-weary sophistication. Indeed, only "Family Album" makes something of a break with tradition. Gathered in the parental home after the funeral of their father, the Featherways reminisce about their childhood. Thanks to an ample supply of madeira and to the relief felt at the passing of the family tyrant, they finally reveal their hatred of their father, all to the ironic accompaniment of simple, sentimental music box melodies. But "Family Album" is more an anecdote than a play, and the music is incidental.

What is true of the subject matter is also true of the writing in general. Except for some reticence about expressing deep emo-

tional feeling, a reticence even more pronounced in and typical of
Coward's non-musical plays, the dialogue contains little that is
distinctive. Here, for example, is part of the first scene in *Bitter-
Sweet* between Sarah, a well-to-do English girl, soon to be mar-
ried, and Carl, her music teacher, who is foreign and very poor.
She has just finished singing one of his songs:

Carl: We have festivals in the spring in my country—and the young
boys and girls dance and their clothes are brightly colored, glinting
in the sun, and the old people sit round under the trees, watching and
tapping their sticks on the ground and reviving in their hearts memories
of when they, too, were young and in love.

Sarah: In love.

Carl: Yes—as you are in love with your handsome Mr. Devon.

Sarah: Oh—Hugh—yes, of course. Tell me more about your country, Mr. Linden.

Carl: There is nothing to tell really—it seems so very far away—
I've almost forgotten.

Sarah: You're homesick though, I can see you are.

Carl: Can you?

Sarah: Perhaps it's the climate here, it *is* depressing—

Carl: Yes, a little [*He sings*]:
> Tho' there may be beauty in this land of yours,
>   Skies are very often dull and grey;
> If I could but take that little hand of yours,
>   Just to lead you secretly away.°

Who would be surprised if this were presented as an excerpt from
an operetta by Franz Lehar or Rudolf Friml or any one of a dozen
similar writers?

The love songs share the same sentimental traditions. Coward
says of "The Mirabelle Waltz" that it "was really written as a satire on the popular musical comedy waltzes of the period, i.e.,
1900. The words are deliberately trite and so is the tune. . . ." [4]
Here is part of the refrain:

> All my life I have been waiting,
> Dreaming ages through;
> Until today I suddenly discover
> The form and face of he who is my lover.

No more tears and hesitating,
Fate has sent me you.
Time and tide can never sever
Those whom love has bound forever,
Dear lover of my Dreams come true.

The rhyme on "waiting" and "hesitating" is certainly less than graceful, and a line like "Time and tide can never sever" is certainly trite; but are these lines so very different from the following from *Private Lives,* one of Coward's most acrid comedies?

Someday I'll find you, moonlight behind you,
True to the dream I am dreaming.
As I draw near you you'll smile a little smile;
For a little while we shall stand hand in hand.
I'll leave you never, love you forever,
All our past sorrow redeeming; try to make it true,
Say you love me too.
Someday I'll find you again.

The point need not be stressed any further. Insofar as story line and romantic music and lyrics are concerned, Coward in his musical plays is at one with the Edwardian operetta writers of his youth; in fact, except for *Sail Away* and *Ace of Clubs,* Coward deliberately harks back to older styles instead of using some of the more recent styles and subject matter.

IV *Comic Songs*

The comic songs reveal something a little more distinctively Cowardian and original, although his indebtedness to earlier writers, particularly W. S. Gilbert, is apparent. Set to vivacious but basically simple tunes, "Mad Dogs and Englishmen," "Mrs. Worthington," "The Stately Homes of England," and "Don't Let's be Beastly to the Germans," to mention only a few of the best known, are patter songs comparable to Gilbert and Sullivan's "Here's a Howdy-Do," "A Policeman's Lot is not A Happy One," or "My Name is John Wellington Wells." There is the same demand on the singer to enunciate cascades of consonants, the same play with internal rhymes, the same shifts from formality to bathos, and the same prickling satiric tone.

But Coward lacks Gilbert's metrical ingenuity. His song lyrics cannot stand very well separately as poems since shifts in rhythm, emphasis, and line length become meaningful only in connection with the music. His songs, even the most comic patter songs, are not *set* to music; words and music take form together. Another difference from Gilbert is that Coward's comic songs rarely grow out of a clear dramatic context; they are numbers tailored to suit the abilities and personalities of certain performers. Some songs, notably "Mrs. Worthington" and "Don't Let's be Beastly to the Germans," were not written for any production at all, and have been sung almost exclusively by Coward himself. He has also, as it were, taken back some songs which were first performed by others, especially "Mad Dogs and Englishmen."

Another whose repertoire depends a good deal on material written for her by Coward is Beatrice Lillie. Surely some of the comic songs should outlast Coward, Miss Lillie, and the other Coward beneficiaries, just as some of the sentimental waltz songs have long since become part of the body of popular music.

V *Assessment*

An evaluation of Noel Coward's work in the musical theater must take two kinds of material into account, the sentimental-romantic and the satiric. In neither area can Coward be called an innovator, yet in both he has produced works of exemplary polish and élan. At present it seems that only individual songs have the power to survive, though possibly *Bitter-Sweet* and *Conversation Piece* might be revived by light opera companies, in the way that some of the operettas of Offenbach and Strauss have been successfully revived recently. Coward's music is less substantial than theirs, but his plots are as good or better. For English and American audiences his libretti have the advantage of having originally been written in literate English, which puts them well ahead of even the best translations and adaptations from other languages. However, since his operettas are not basically comic, as are those of Gilbert and Sullivan, the question the producer will have to ask is whether their romantic sentiments have become sufficiently old-fashioned to be quaint and charming.

CHAPTER 3

"Just the echo of a sigh"

THERE is a familiar photograph of Noel Coward by Mark Swain[1] that comes about as close as any single item could to capturing the most popular image of the man. Dressed in a dinner jacket (the photograph almost whispers "impeccably dressed"), Coward stands in a fashionable slouch, left hand in jacket pocket, the thumb outside the pocket, a king-sized cigarette in a long, silver-trimmed holder in the raised right hand, and his head is tilted back. There is a carnation in the lapel buttonhole and an impressive triangle of handkerchief above the breast pocket. The smile is not quite there. Sophistication, aplomb, polish, and a touch of insolence—all these, and more, seem embodied here. How gratifying that the author of *Private Lives*, of *Design for Living*, and of *Present Laughter* should really look the part. When he appears on the stage in a Las Vegas night club dressed like this, who would mistake him for anybody else? In any final evaluation of Coward's work, this suave figure must take first place; but there are other Noel Cowards, at least one of whom is a far more serious, although hardly somber, figure.

Coward as composer, as performer, and, pre-eminently, as the writer of comedy has overshadowed the writer of serious plays. He has written over a dozen such works, many of which were very successful in production and some of which must be rated equally successful artistically within the narrow limits of their intentions. It is, however, that very narrowness of intention and of subject matter which makes the serious plays less important than the comedies and makes a consideration of the serious plays a logical prelude to a discussion of the comedies. The comedies are not only superior as a whole, but they often show Coward's limitations as a serious dramatist converted into assets. But "less important" does not mean "unimportant." Coward's skills are as evident and as impressive in *Cavalcade* as in *Blithe Spirit*, and *Still Life* is

a beautifully constructed one-act play. Yet, while skill can in itself
be a major source of delight in a comedy, it is expected to serve
some larger purpose if a serious play is to demand attention beyond the moment of reading or performance. Coward has rarely
attempted to deal with such larger purposes, and it is this more
than anything that gives his serious work, for all its polish and
theatrical power, a secondary but very respectable place.

Coward's serious plays range from the already mentioned Ruritanian melodrama in *The Queen Was in the Parlour* to the quiet,
realistic vignettes of *Still Life;* from the psychological drama of
The Vortex, almost classical in maintaining the unities, to the
panorama of *Cavalcade.* What they have in common is best explained in negative terms. Although many end unhappily, they
have nothing of the tragic about them either in intent or in execution; few of them aim at eliciting more than a quiet sob or, as
Coward put it in the song "I'll See You Again," "just the echo of a
sigh." Although some deal with situations that an Ibsen or a Shaw
might have used to demonstrate or argue questions of public morality or political philosophy, only *Post-Mortem* (significantly the
only one of Coward's published plays never to have been performed) can be said to have a thesis. And, although all these plays
are realistic in the sense of accepting the conventions of the fourth
wall, of representational scenery, of careful attention to the passage of time, and of the logical, plausible plot, Coward rarely
comes to terms on a deeper level with his characters in the way of
the Realistic playwright like Ibsen, Chekov, or Arthur Miller—
instead, each character is conceived of in comic terms, that is, two-
dimensionally, more as an embodiment of certain premises rather
than as an individual with individual motivation.

I   The Vortex

Quite different conclusions were forecast when *The Vortex* appeared in 1924. Although it was not the first Coward play to be
produced, it was the first to capture both public and critical ac-
claim; and the history of its first production is almost the prototype of the story of the new, serious playwright. Norman Macdermott had, in 1920, converted "an old drill hall in Hampstead into
what was, by 1924, the flourishing try-out and repertory theatre,
the Everyman." Coward submitted some plays to him; and, although Macdermott tended to prefer *Hay Fever,* "as there was no

good part for me in that, I managed to sheer him over to *The Vortex.*" [2]

The road to opening night was strewn with obstacles. Initial casting was difficult because the rule at the Everyman was that all actors appeared at a fixed salary of five pounds a week; the theater depended, therefore, on actors who were willing to take a chance on appearing in a success that could be moved to the West End where salaries would revert to normal. And this unpleasant play by a virtually unknown playwright looked to many suspiciously like a failure. Once casting was finally completed, Macdermott revealed that the play would have to be abandoned unless an additional two hundred pounds were raised; but Coward turned to Michael Arlen, whose *The Green Hat* had just become a best seller, and raised the money. Then one of the leading actresses developed diphtheria and had to be replaced; and, even more serious, Kate Cutler, for whom Coward had written the role of the mother, became incensed about the way Coward had enlarged his own part, that of Nicky, in rewriting the last act, and resigned from the cast a week before the opening. In desperation, Coward turned to Lilian Braithwaite, an actress he greatly admired but who seemed to most people, especially to Macdermott, completely wrong for the role. Nonetheless, she was engaged. But Coward had other difficulties:

Meanwhile, I was having a spirited duel with the Lord Chamberlain (Lord Cromer) in his office in St. James's. He had at first refused point-blank to grant a licence for the play because of the unpleasantness of its theme, and it was only after a long-drawn-out argument, during which, I must say, he was charming and sympathetic, that I persuaded him that the play was little more than a moral tract. With a whimsical and rather weary smile he finally granted the licence. . . .[3]

The licence was granted only a few hours before the opening on November 25, 1924; and the favorable response of the audience proved that all the agony and confusion had been well worth it. *The Vortex* played at the Everyman for twelve performances, and then moved to the West End for another two hundred and twenty-four. The next fall Coward appeared in the play in New York, where it was received with equal enthusiasm.

The Vortex, a mixture of Ibsen and Maugham, has also a strong suggestion of *Hamlet* in the play's ancestry. Florence Lancaster, who is probably in her fifties, is motivated by a desire to remain young-looking, physically desirable, and adored by all. She is having an affair with Tom Veryan, the latest of the young men who have helped her retain illusions about her youth and beauty. Her husband, David, who has long since retreated into the background, manages his farm and closes his eyes to his wife's behavior. Their son, Nicky, twenty-four, returns from a year of music study in Paris and announces that he is tentatively engaged to Bunty Mainwaring. Florence conceals her concern and invites Bunty to a weekend house party.

There Bunty and Tom, who had known each other before, fall in love; Florence discovers them kissing, and against a background of wild jazz played by Nicky at the piano, she hysterically orders the two young people out of her house. In the last act, mother and son confront each other. He gets her to confess that her young men have been more to her than handsome escorts, and he confesses that he has been taking dope. The play ends with both promising to try to be different, but the future looks bleak. Nicky says early in the last act: "To-morrow morning I shall see things quite differently. That's true—that's the tragedy of it, and you won't see. To-morrow morning I *shall* see things quite differently. All this will seem unreal—a nightmare—the machinery of our lives will go on again and gloss over the truth as it always does—and our chance will be gone forever." The chance is *not* lost; nonetheless, the character of the mother makes the possibility of profound reform unlikely.

The form of the play is that of *Ghosts;* indeed, the final moments of *The Vortex,* where mother and son are alone on the stage and all illusions are shattered, are more than just an echo of Ibsen's play. Florence Lancaster's plight is not so desperate as Mrs. Alving's, but there is clearly the same sense of the abyss open before the heroine's feet: "She sits quite still, staring in front of her—the tears are rolling down her cheeks, and she is stroking Nicky's hair mechanically in an effort to calm him."

The style, however, is more like Maugham's. Especially in the first act, the tone is witty and flippant. Most of the exposition is carried by Helen and Pauncefort (called "Pawnie"), two of Florence's most sophisticated friends; and they introduce the two central characters and suggest the nature of the theme:

Pawnie: I expect Florence will just go on and on, then suddenly become quite beautifully old, and go on and on still more.

Helen: It's too late now for her to become beautifully old, I'm afraid. She'll have to be young indefinitely.

Pawnie: I don't suppose she'll mind that, but it's trying for David.

Helen: And fiendish for Nicky.

Pawnie: Oh, no, my dear; you're quite wrong there. I'm sure Nicky doesn't care a damn.

. . . . .

Helen: He only takes things seriously in spurts, but still he's very young.

Pawnie: Do you really think that's a good excuse?

Helen: No, I'm afraid not, especially when so much depends on it.

Pawnie: What does depend on it?

Helen: Everything—his life's happiness.

Pawnie: Don't be so terribly intense, dear. . . .

. . . . .

Helen: He may have had everything he wanted, but he's had none of the things he really needs.

Pawnie: Are you talking socially or spiritually?

Helen: You're quite right, Pawnie, you wouldn't be so beautifully preserved if you'd wasted any of your valuable time on sincerity.

Compared with Maugham's *The Constant Wife,* for example, Coward's characters are drawn more broadly; and the insults are more obvious and cruel. The question is just how successfully Coward can modulate from such a brittle tone into one more suitable for the revelations and recognitions of the last act.

Pawnie's comment, "Don't be so terribly intense," reveals his callous dilettantism but is also a justifiable deflation of Helen's oracular, but trite comment. Something similar can be said for much of the third act; while the son is intent on lacerating his mother's conscience, the language lags behind:

Nicky: You ran after him up the stairs because your vanity wouldn't let you lose him. It isn't that you love him—that would be easier—you never love anyone, you only love them loving you—all your so-called passion and temperament is false—your whole existence has degenerated into an endless empty craving for admiration and flattery—and then you say you've done no harm to anybody. Father used to be a clever man, with a strong will and a capacity for enjoying everything —I can remember him like that—and now he's nothing—a complete nonentity because his spirit's crushed. How could it be otherwise?

You've let him down consistently for years—and God knows I'm nothing for him to look forward to—but I might have been if it hadn't been
for you—

Florence: Don't talk like that. Don't—don't. It can't be such a crime
being loved—it can't be such a crime being happy—

Nicky: You're not happy—you're never happy—you're fighting—
fighting all the time to keep your youth and your looks—because you
can't bear the thought of living without them—as though they mattered
in the end.

Florence [hysterically]: What does anything matter—ever?

The weakness of these speeches is apparent: they are impressive but full of empty abstractions. Too much sounds like the author's résumé rather than the passionate outcry of a son who has,
in the course of an hour, been jilted by his fiancée, discovered his
mother's adultery, and realized the true nature of his mother's
character and the disastrous effect it has had on both his father
and himself.

Of course, language alone is not at fault; for an author's style is
inseparable from his whole approach to character and situation.
Coward has said, "My original motive in *The Vortex* was to write
a good play with a whacking good part in it for myself, and I am
thankful to say, with a few modest reservations, that I succeeded." [4] Certainly the role of Nicky has a great deal to offer a
performer, particularly a young one who cares little for subtleties
and much for powerful effects. Nicky is the equal of any character
in his ability to trade witty insults, yet he has an anguished soul
beneath; he is a competent pianist; he is a dope addict; he is in
love; he is a doting son; and finally, he must face the painful, but
ever-so-theatrical task of castigating his own beloved mother.

To Coward it seemingly does not matter that all is not equally
clear or convincing. What, for example, is the nature of the relationship between Nicky and Bunty? Coward keeps the action
moving fast, shifts masks quickly; and somehow the impression of
a complex character is created. The mother's role is almost as
tempting to an actress; but, like Nicky's, it is only a "whacking
good part." They are not convincing, full-drawn characters; and
some of the others—the father, for example—are hardly characters at all, and exist only because tangible actors are on stage.

Nonetheless, considering the author's age and the general situation of the English theater in 1924, *The Vortex* deserved its suc-

cess, as well as the hope that Coward was a new playwright from whom much could be expected. Aside from Shaw, there were few British playwrights whose work went beyond fairly conventional melodrama and light comedy, and none of these was so young, so clever, and so shocking as Coward. None of the new plays had the immediacy and nervous energy of *The Vortex,* which seemed to go to the very heart of modern decadence and corruption (and decadence among the upper classes always seems more shocking than elsewhere); nor had anyone before Coward had the audacity to make such a sympathetic display of dope addiction, gigolos, and mother-baiting. And none of the new plays came from such an impressive young man—author, actor, director, composer, and, thanks to the machinery of publicity, bon vivant.

Following *The Vortex,* Coward produced, in rapid succession, a new revue, *On With the Dance* (1925); two new comedies, *Fallen Angels* and *Hay Fever* (both 1925); a Ruritanian melodrama, *The Queen Was in the Parlour* (1926); and another serious play, *Easy Virtue* (New York, 1925; London, 1926). Most of these, except for the revue, are works that were substantially completed before *The Vortex* was produced. All were not greeted with equal enthusiasm, but Coward's stock remained high. His ability to extract a maximum of theatrical power from meager materials was undeniable.

II Easy Virtue

In the opening scene of *Easy Virtue* (1925), the Whittakers— the Colonel, Mrs. Whittaker, and their two daughters, Marion and Hilda—await the arrival of John, the only son, who has recently married a woman they have never met. When John arrives, his wife, Larita, proves to be an extremely elegant woman, older than John, and, to the Whittakers' dismay, divorced. Although Colonel Whittaker treats Larita kindly, the other members of the family are cold. Larita is dreadfully bored; John's hearty dedication to tennis and other outdoor sports revolts her; and the hatred emanating from the other women grows more intense daily. The situation comes to a head three months later, and the climax is precipitated by Hilda's discovery of a newspaper account of a suicide fifteen years earlier in which Larita seems to have had some responsibility.

Hilda's revelation of this story causes a quarrel in which Larita

charges Marion with prudery and repressed desires, and Mrs.
Whittaker orders Larita to spend the evening in her room, although this is the evening when the Whittakers are giving a
dance. At the height of the dance, Larita appears, extravagantly
dressed and bejeweled. She explains to Sarah Hurst, John's childhood sweetheart, that she is going away and asks Sarah to take
care of John, implying that Sarah and John should soon be able to
marry. Then, telling no one about her intentions, she walks out to
her waiting car; and the curtain falls.

Coward's own comments on the play deserve to be quoted almost in full:

From the 'eighties onwards until the outbreak of the 1914–18 War
the London theatre was enriched by a series of plays, notably by
Somerset Maugham or Arthur Pinero, which were described as "drawing-room dramas." I suppose that the apotheosis of these was *The Second
Mrs. Tanqueray*, but there were many others. . . . All of these
"drawing-room dramas" dealt with the psychological and social problems of the upper middle classes. The characters in them were, as a
general rule, wealthy, well-bred, articulate and motivated by the exigencies of the world to which they belonged. This world was snobbish,
conventional, polite, and limited by its own codes and rules of behavior,
and it was the contravention of these codes and rules—to our eyes so
foolish and old-fashioned—that supplied the dramatic content of most
of the plays I have mentioned. The heroine of *His House in Order*
[Pinero] rebelled against the narrow pomposities of the family into
which she had married. Lady Frederick [in Maugham's play of the
same name], by gallantly and daringly exposing the secrets of her
dressing-table, deflected the attentions of a young man who was in-
fatuated by her into a more suitable alliance. In a recent revival of the
play, this scene still proved to be dramatically impeccable. The unhappy Paula Tanqueray tried valiantly to live down her earlier moral
turpitude, but ultimately gave up the struggle and perished offstage
in an aura of righteous atonement, just before the final curtain. It is
easy nowadays to laugh at these vanished moral attitudes, but they
were poignant enough in their time because they were true. Those
high-toned drawing-room histrionics are over and done with. Women
with pasts to-day receive far more enthusiastic social recognition than
women without pasts. The narrow-mindedness, the moral righteousness,
and the over-rigid social codes have disappeared, but with them have
gone much that was graceful, well-behaved, and endearing. It was in
a mood of nostalgic regret at the decline of such conventions that I
wrote *Easy Virtue*. When it was produced, several critics triumphantly

pounced on the fact that the play was similar in form and tone and plot to the plays of Pinero. I myself was unimpressed by their perception, for the form and tone and plot of a Pinero play was exactly what I had tried to achieve.[5]

This passage is very curious indeed. What is said about the pre-war "drawing-room dramas" is well and sympathetically said and is another sign of how thoroughly Coward is himself a product of those years although most of his plays present an up-to-date mask to the world. However, the relevance of the last few sentences to *Easy Virtue* is a bit difficult to find; for what conventions are viewed nostalgically? Certainly what little there is in the play of the "graceful, the well-behaved and the endearing" belongs to the woman with a past, not to the narrow-minded society in which she feels herself trapped. Anyway, "the narrow-mindedness, the moral righteousness, and the over-rigid social codes" have certainly not disappeared, if the Whittaker household is in any way representative; in fact, with the aid of some simple Freudian formulations, Coward demonstrates that these attitudes have not only remained but have grown more sinister since they take their origins in twisted psyches rather than in "the exigencies of the world" to which the characters belong. Could this, perhaps, have been his point, that what was once acceptable because it had social approval has become ugly when it is the manifestation of the dark subconscious? If this is the source of "nostalgic regret," the play is a rather oblique way of presenting it. Only one thing is quite accurate; "the form and tone and plot" are certainly those of a Pinero play.

Easy Virtue is "*The Second Mrs. Tanqueray* brought down to date,"[6] and *The Vortex* turned upside down. Except for Colonel Whittaker who, like the father in *The Vortex,* represents solid sensibleness, and Sarah Hurst, a well-balanced young woman, all the positive values lie with Larita and her world. Yet how does it differ from Florence Lancaster's world? Larita is presented as generous and broad-minded, well-read, and well-informed, and as having as her only illusion the belief that she could find contentment with John; but the Whittaker women are presented as provincial, narrow-minded, repressed, and emasculating.

But Mrs. Whittaker and Marion are caricatures, and Larita's depth must be taken too much on faith. Larita's conversations

with Charles Burleigh, the only person who "talks her language,"
are trivial and gossipy; and her past, presented in veiled terms,
justifies James Agate's statement that in this play Coward "has
attained to that pure idealism which prompts the schoolboy who
has been taken to see La Dame aux Camelias to believe for the
next ten years that a cocotte is the noblest work of man if not of
God." [7]

Coward charges that Jane Cowl, who played Larita both in
New York and in London, distorted the play by stressing its tragic
rather than its comic overtones and by responding to the Whittakers with deep emotion rather than with exasperation. To the
reader, however, these distinctions do not alter the basic nature of
the play. What Coward most regretted about the passing of the
Pinero-type play, it would seem, was not the actual world it may
have mirrored, but the opportunity for striking black and white
contrasts and for more "whacking good" parts.

III   The Queen Was in the Parlour

The Queen Was in the Parlour (1926) exploits yet another
source of theatrical excitement, pure hokum. Nadya, the widow of
the Archduke Alexander of Krayia, as an expatriate in Paris has
found true love with Sabien Pastal, whom she plans to marry. Her
peace is shattered by the arrival of General Krish who brings the
news of the assassination of the king of Krayia, for Nadya must
return to be their queen. Reluctantly, she writes a letter of farewell to Sabien and leaves for Krayia. A year later, on the eve of
Nadya's marriage to Prince Keri of Zalgar, Sabien finds his way to
her, asks to spend one last night, and Nadya agrees. Unfortunately, it is also the night chosen by dissident forces in Krayia to
begin a revolution. General Krish and Prince Keri try to get
Nadya to escape, but she, *en negligée*, faces the crowd from her
balcony, tells them to shoot her—if they have the courage—and,
with Prince Keri beside her, recaptures the people's loyalty. There
is a shot in Nadya's bedroom, and General Krish enters, saying
"Your Majesty, a man has been shot trying to get in at your window." Thus, both the peace of Krayia and Nadya's honor are preserved; somehow, adultery before the coronation and a wedding
doesn't count.

Despite some moments of comedy and some clever, tongue-in-
cheek allusions to the fountainhead of Ruritanian romance, An-

thony Hope's *The Prisoner of Zenda,* Coward's play is meant to be taken seriously. This effect may still be possible for a certain audience for whom royal figures exist in a rarefied atmosphere, but *The Queen Was in the Parlour* must now seem dated and inane to most people.

IV Sirocco

In *Sirocco*—originally written in 1921, but considerably rewritten before it was produced in 1927—the heroine is Lucy, a good-looking, naturally quiet Englishwoman still in her early twenties. She has been married for three years to Stephen Griffin, an unimaginative, thoroughly conventional executive in an oil company. As the play opens, he is leaving for some weeks in Tunis, but he stolidly refuses to let Lucy go with him, insisting that she will be much better off with his mother and the rest of the English colony in Bellagualia, an Italian Riviera resort. His inability to comprehend Lucy's boredom with the smug, parochial English group not only intensifies her irritation and despair but leaves her open to the suave advances of Sirio Marson, a painter of mixed Italian and English ancestry, and a polished philanderer.

At a local *festa,* where the English behave more fatuously than ever, Lucy succumbs to Sirio's advances; and they go to his studio in Florence. A week later, Lucy finds that most of the glamor has evaporated; she is appalled by Sirio's slovenly habits, his amorality, his refusal to think beyond the pleasures of the moment. While Sirio is out, Lucy has a visit from her husband and mother-in-law. Stephen "magnanimously" offers Lucy the chance to return to him, but his motives are transparently selfish. Lucy sends the Griffins away; but, when Sirio returns, she finds his hedonism as repulsive as her husband's respectability. They quarrel and come to blows; Sirio storms out; and Lucy, just before the curtain: "[*suddenly lifts her arms above her head. With exultance*]: I'm free—free for the first time in my life. [*Her face changes.*] God help me! [*She leans on the table and buries her head in her arms.*]"

Sirocco was possibly the most thorough failure of Coward's career. On the opening night, the audience received the first act dully, but in the middle of the second act "the storm broke" during the love scene: "The gallery shrieked with mirth and made sucking sounds when he kissed her, and from then onwards proceeded to punctuate every line with catcalls and various other animal noises. The last act was chaos from beginning to end. The gallery, upper circle, and pit hooted and yelled, while the stalls, boxes, and dress circle whispered and shushed. Most of the lines weren't heard at all. . . . The curtain finally fell amid a bedlam of sound. . . ." [8]

Coward suspected that the demonstration had been organized by enemies, and he may well have been right since it is difficult now to understand what in the play could have created such a response. Although the execution falters, the basic outline has a good deal to recommend it. Indeed, St. John Ervine found the moral substance of the play impressive:

Mr. Coward has, in short, written a tract. *This*, he says in effect, is what all this cinema romance amounts to, something foul and sluttish and finally impossible. Routine affection may be, and no doubt is, devastatingly dull, but vamp-love, movie-passion—these are duller still, and those who mistake Hollywood for heaven are likely to land in hell. I protest against the assumption, now too commonly made, that Mr. Coward is a flippant youth who delights in the pretence that vice is virtue. The faults in this play are numerous . . . but all these faults are the faults of a young mind, made excessively indignant by what it conceives to be wrongs and injustices. His sincerity is transparent, and his motives . . . are generous.[9]

In 1927, just a year after Rudolph Valentino's death, the comments about movie passion were surely more apropos than they seem to be now; and Ivor Novello, who played Sirio, looks, in the photographs of the production, as if a resemblance to Valentino might well have been intended. The fact that Novello was already a popular movie actor also may have influenced Ervine to see the play as a commentary on the movies, but to the reader today this limits the play unnecessarily. Ervine is right, however, in seeing that the basic nature of the play is moral and realistic. In fact, the audience's outrage is surely traceable in part to its refusal to accept the possibility of such things being true of a proper young Englishwoman.

The difficulty with *Sirocco* lies, as it does in *The Vortex* and in *Easy Virtue*, in the basically theatrical nature of the characters and the situation. Neither Lucy nor Sirio is clearly defined except insofar as conventional and abstract labels can be affixed. Lucy is young, beautiful, romantic, and, in the language of the sentimental novel, ready to be swept off her feet (but what has her life with her husband been like for the last three years? And why three years, except that for Coward this seems always to represent the outer limits of passion?). Sirio is the passionate Latin, magnetic and amoral.

These labels are hardly different in kind from those applicable to the minor characters, who are more reasonably stereotypes: Stephen is the stolid oaf; his mother, the dignified, but narrow-minded dowager; Francine Trott, the hearty, overgrown schoolgirl; the Reverend Crutch, the complacent minister. Appropriate enough for comedy, and perhaps not altogether as stereotyped in 1927 as novelists and playwrights were to make them before that decade was over, these characters are hardly enough to carry the weight of a serious analysis of love and passion.

The same criticism applies to the situations. The *festa* in the second act is drawn in primary colors; the cold English are prudish and patronizing; and the hot-blooded Italians are uninhibited and "natural." With the aid of liberal servings of Asti, Sirio draws Lucy into his world, but not before Coward has invoked the *deus ex machina*. Sirio bravely stops a violent fight, is himself stabbed in the hand, and his bravery and injury combine to destroy Lucy's defenses. In the last act, another *deus* appears: a letter from Sirio's mother. Sirio's stepfather has run off with *his* mistress, and the mother wants Sirio home. Coming when it does, this letter conveniently serves to reinforce Lucy's disgust with the world into which she has wandered, helps to illuminate her finer moral character, and quickly gets Sirio off the stage and out of Lucy's life. In short, the plot progresses through coincidence rather than character.

Finally, the dialogue does not have the nervous energy, the mixture of wit and brutality, that keeps *The Vortex* afloat. Since the characters are quite outside the milieu with which Coward usually deals, the dialogue, both comic and serious, must also be on a much less sophisticated level. This play is fine so long as it concerns itself with pictures of the self-satisfied English abroad; but when Coward is faced by the problem of presenting his Latin lover, he oscillates between making Marson impressively fluent and comically inept. For example, when Sirio's seductive powers are approaching their peak, he speaks like this: "You are like a deep pool in the rocks—nothing moving—very cool and still—but there is a little channel you know nothing about, and one day you will be taken by surprise. The great sea will come swirling in froth and foam and coloured bubbles, and you will be stirred to your depths—strange forces you never realized will be dragged to the surface. I am warning you."

A week later, after passion has run its course and disillusion has set in, his fluency has diminished: "You are being capable—I hate you when you are capable. You are making the better of a bad job, eh? Rising to an occasion. For God's sake stop and let us both sit and scream." As for Lucy, in climactic moments she, like Nicky in *The Vortex*, resorts to speeches of analysis where something more powerful is called for:

[To her husband when he asks her to return with him:] No, no—don't go—I must make you see—I want to make you understand that I'm sorry, really sorry for having upset you and made things difficult, but it's not as serious and important as you think it is—really and truly it isn't, because you don't love me, Stephen; you never have really, and I don't love you. We were silly to marry, and it's been a failure, it's no life for either of us just existing on and on without warmth until we're old—we're miles apart and always have been. Don't look like that, I'm not talking nonsense—it's from my heart all this—I want you to see— I want you to see—. . . . Let me speak—you must, this is probably the last time we shall ever see each other, and you must listen to me. If you had loved me, really loved me, this could never have happened— that's not an excuse, it's the truth.

Perhaps in real life a Lucy might talk like this, but on the stage how very stale, flat and unprofitable her words sound.

V Post-Mortem

Sirocco opened in London on November 24, 1927, and created for the moment a pause in Coward's mounting success and reputation. However, the next two years saw his career move forward with astonishing vigor. In January, 1928, he appeared in the leading role of the London production of S. N. Behrman's *The Second Man;* in March of that year, his revue, *This Year of Grace,* opened in London; in October, *This Year of Grace* opened in New York, with Coward in the cast; in July, 1929, *Bitter-Sweet* opened in London; in November, the American company of *Bitter-Sweet* opened in New York. All of these were, in the press agent's word, "triumphs." When, on November 29, 1929, Coward set sail from San Francisco for a leisurely holiday in the Orient, the disaster of *Sirocco* was ancient history. On his return to England some months later, he had three interesting items in his luggage; an unfinished and soon to be discarded novel, *Julian Kane;* the completed script for *Private Lives;* and "an angry little vilification of war called *Post-Mortem*."

The genesis of *Post-Mortem* (1933) is outlined in *Present Indicative*. In Singapore, Coward had appeared as Stanhope in *Journey's End* as "an amusing experiment" and to help out a touring company called "The Quaints." On the boat from Ceylon to Marseilles, he says, "my mind was strongly affected by *Journey's End* and I had read several current war novels one after the other." Coward does not mention which war novels he had been reading, those like *A Farewell to Arms* and *All Quiet on the Western Front*—both published in 1929, and along with *Journey's End* part of a strong and fashionable movement to debunk war—or more sentimental work. In either case, Coward is concerned in his play with stressing two points: first, that life twelve years after the war is more empty, mindless and corrupt than ever; and, second, the chief proof of this state is that very few can face the truth about the war itself.

The play is cast in a mold of semi-fantasy. The first scene takes place in "a company headquarters in a quiet section of the Front Line in the spring of 1917." Discussion is stimulated by a particularly offensive item in the *Mercury*, a tabloid published by John Cavan's father; the item is an open letter to England, "I Gave My Son," by Lady Stagg-Mortimer. Cavan, as disgusted as the rest, is hopeful that after the war is over the public will eventually know the truth. Perry Lomas, a poet, is pessimistic: "Never, never, never! They'll never know whichever way it goes, victory or defeat. They'll smarm it all over with memorials and Rolls of Honour and Angels of Mons, and it'll look so noble and glorious in retrospect that they'll all start itching for another war, egged on by deaf old gentlemen in clubs who wish they were twenty years younger, and newspaper owners and oily financiers, and the splendid women of England happy and proud to give their sons and husbands and lovers, and even their photographs."

John Cavan, who refuses to accept such a dark view, insists that "something will come out of it" and that he's "treading water, waiting to see": "I have a feeling that one might see the whole business just for a second before one dies. Like going under an anaesthetic, everything becomes blurred and enormous and then suddenly clears, just for the fraction of a fraction of a moment. Perhaps that infinitesimal moment is what we're all waiting for, really." That "fraction of a fraction of a moment" occupies most of the rest of the play. A few minutes after making this speech, John goes out on a patrol. He is hit and carried back to the shelter; in his last moments of life, he finds himself projected forward into 1930.

Six scenes are devoted to John Cavan's visit to 1930. In the first and last he is with his mother; between these two scenes he calls on Monica, his former fiancée; then on Perry Lomas, who has recently published a book on the war which has caused considerable dismay; then goes to the offices of the *Mercury*, where his father has assembled a group of distinguished citizens who call for having Perry's book burned; and finally attends a dinner party with three of the officers who were with Cavan in France. His mother warns John at their first meeting that "There's nothing, nothing worth finding out," and the other scenes become increasingly painful as John realizes how true Perry's prophecy was. In the very last scene, back at John's deathbed, he opens his eyes and says, "You were right, Perry—a poor joke!"

In *Post-Mortem* Coward *has* written a tract in which Perry Lomas, the poet, has the key speech:

Nothing's happening, really. There are strides being made forward in science and equal sized strides being made backwards in hypocrisy. People are just the same: individually pleasant and collectively idiotic. Machinery is growing magnificently, people paint pictures of it and compose ballets about it, the artists are cottoning on to that very quickly because they're scared that soon there won't be any other sort of beauty left, and they'll be stranded with nothing to paint and nothing to write. Religion is doing very well. The Catholic Church still tops the bill as far as finance and general efficiency go. The Church of England is still staggering along without much conviction. . . . Christian Science is coming up smiling, a slightly superior smile, but always a smile. God is Love, there is no pain, Pain is error. Everything that isn't Love is error; like hell it is. Politically all is confusion, but that's nothing new. There's still poverty, unemployment, pain, greed, cruelty, passion, and crime. There's still meanness, jealousy, money, and disease. The competitive sporting spirit is being admirably fostered, particularly as regards the Olympic Games. A superb preparation for the next war, fully realized by everyone but the public that will be involved. The newspapers still lie over anything of importance, and the majority still believes them implicitly. The only real difference in post-war conditions is that there are so many women whose heartache will never heal. The rest is the same, only faster and more meretricious. The war is fashionable now, like a pleasantly harrowing film. . . . Go back to your mother for the time that's left, say good-bye to her, be sweet to her as you're sweet to everybody and just a little sweeter; that may be worth something, although it passes in a flash. . . . Hold close to your own love wherever it lies, don't leave it lonely while you wander about aimlessly in chaos searching for some half-formulated ideal. An ideal of what? Fundamental good in human nature! Bunk! Spiritual understanding? Bunk! God in some compassionate dream waiting to open your eyes to truth? Bunk! Bunk! Bunk! It's all a joke with nobody to laugh at it.

Perry ends the scene by killing himself.

The despair is close to complete, and *Post-Mortem* goes far beyond being merely "an angry little vilification of war." If anything, it is the peace which is vilified; war is seen as having some value in itself:

John: Have you completely forgotten that strange feeling we had in the war? Have you found anything in your lives since to equal it in strength? A sort of splendid carelessness it was, holding us together. Cut off from everything we were used to, but somehow not lonely, except when we were on leave, or when letters came. Depending only upon the immediate moment. No past, no future, and no conviction of God. God died early in the war, for most of us. Can you remember our small delights? How exciting they were? Sleep, warmth, food, drink, unexpected comforts snatched out of turmoil, so simple in enjoyment, and so incredibly satisfying.

Coward's own comments on *Post-Mortem* strike a note of humility:

I wrote *Post-Mortem* with the utmost sincerity; this, I think, must be fairly obvious to anyone who reads it. In fact, I tore my emotions to shreds over it. The result was similar to my performance as Stanhope: confused, underrehearsed, and hysterical. Unlike my performance as

Stanhope, however, it had some very fine moments. There is, I believe, some of the best writing I have ever done in it, also some of the worst. I have no deep regrets over it, as I know my intentions to have been of the purest. I passionately believed in the truth of what I was writing: too passionately. . . . Through lack of detachment and lack of real experience of my subject, I muddled the issues of the play. I might have done better had I given more time to it and less vehemence. However, it helped to purge my system of certain accumulated acids.[10]

Certainly those speeches which praise the glories and exaltation of brotherhood in battle reflect a lack of experience. Lack of detachment is evident in the scenes with the mother, for these scenes are virtually a parody of the maudlin stiff-upper-lip tradition. But, when Coward attacks post-war hypocrisy, he achieves a high level of satire.

By far the best scene in the play is that in the *Mercury* office. This scene, which at first suggests a revue sketch, soon goes far beyond this suggestion into a Surrealistic, Expressionistic sequence of considerable force; but it is quite out of keeping with the style of the rest of the play. The guiding genius of the scene is Alfred Borrow, city editor, who sees everything in journalistic clichés and distortions. Shortly after meeting John, Borrow begins to turn the moment into a newspaper story: "Return of Sir James Cavan's only son after thirteen years! His mother, a white-haired patrician lady, smiled at our special representative with shining eyes. 'My son,' she said simply. Just that, but in those two words the meed of mother love was welling over." This last device, ascribing volumes of meaning to simple phrases, becomes a dominant motif, virtually a refrain:

"We're out to win," said Sir James Cavan's son smilingly. Just that, but in those simple words what wealth of feeling, what brave, brimming enthusiasm.

"Dad's right," he said. Just two simple words, but, somehow, somehow, one understood.

A technique used persistently in the scene, one reminiscent of the German Expressionists, is that of making all the characters—except John, of course—utterly mechanical. They fail to hear a word John addresses to them; instead, each remains fixed in his own pattern of thought and statement. The climax is reached when

Lady Stagg-Mortimer rises to speak; the secretary produces a typewritten sheet, and "Borrow reads the speech, while Lady Stagg-Mortimer gesticulates and opens and shuts her mouth silently." The scene ends with John's speech praising death, destruction, and despair; and it is set to a background of "God and Country" being chanted "in a monotone, quite softly" by Sir James Cavan, Alfred Borrow, Lady Stagg-Mortimer, Miss Beaver and the Bishop of Ketchworth. Only in this scene is there a successful blending of message and dramatic form. Most of the other scenes—the one with Perry is a partial exception—are static, discursive, and too often extended far beyond the demands of the point being illustrated.

Post-Mortem is an anomaly in the canon of Coward's work. Although its most forceful moments are theatrical in the best sense of the word, Coward insists that it "was not actually written for the theatre"; and there is no record that it has ever been produced. It appears in *Play Parade,* Volume I, published in 1933, as one of "the most representative of my works"; but there are certainly no other Coward plays at all like it; in fact, other works of his dealing with war take quite a different view. Are its dark pessimism and despair "representative"? If such moods play any significant part in Coward's personality, he has done a successful job of keeping them out of his work.

Although one would think at first glance that *Post-Mortem,* presented as a work in which he "had a lot to say," would be a key in discussing Coward's work, the play turns out to be more a sport than a revelation. True, some of the attitudes appear in other places; and the over-all tone might be taken as a deeper, darker version of the disillusionment that lightly shadows the edges of most of Coward's plays. However, *Post-Mortem* makes most sense as a transient phenomenon that is not inconsistent with the main body of his work but is not representative of it.

VI   Cavalcade

Whatever prevented *Post-Mortem* from being produced, it was certainly not any technical difficulty; for few plays call for more elaborate mechanical ingenuity and production finesse than Coward's next play. *Cavalcade* (1931), was quite consciously conceived of as a spectacle for London's Coliseum: "I felt an urge to test my producing powers on a large scale. My mind's eyes visual-

ized a series of tremendous mob scenes—the storming of the Bas-
tille—the massacre of the Huguenots—I believe even the Decline
and Fall of the Roman Empire flirted with me for a little." [11]
After dismissing many such subjects—the Second Empire lingered
longest—Coward came across a bound volume of the *Illustrated
London News;* and the first pictures he saw in it were of a troop-
ship leaving for the Boer War. This stimulated his imagination.
Starting with that scene, Coward wrote a series of scenes covering
the period between New Year's Eve, 1899, and an evening in
1930. The period is almost exactly that of Coward's own life (he
was born a little more than a week before Christmas of 1899);
and at least one episode in the play, the seaside "concert party," is
autobiographical.

The play consists of two interwoven stories, that of the Marryots, an upper-class family (Robert Marryot is knighted about half
way through the play), and that of the Bridges, originally servants to the Marryots, later owners of a pub. Significant moments
in their lives are entwined with important moments of English
history: both Robert Marryot and Alfred Bridges fight in the Boer
War; Robert Marryot has a place in the funeral procession for
Queen Victoria; Edward Marryot and his bride are lost on the
Titanic; Joey Marryot, who has been having an affair with Fanny
Bridges, is lost in World War I. Other scenes take place against
backgrounds reflecting current tastes and activities.

Cavalcade invites a purely statistical discussion: there are
twenty-two scenes, using a total of sixteen settings; the original
program lists forty roles, plus "crowds, soldiers, sailors, guests,
etc."; Coward claims the production required three thousand,
seven hundred costumes; the Drury Lane Theatre, where the play
was eventually presented, needed two new hydraulic lifts to
handle the production (the unavailability of the Coliseum made
Coward dispense with a revolving stage); and, following four
hundred and five performances, *Cavalcade* was made with very
little revision into a highly successful film.

The dramatic scenes occupy only a part of the play, and much
of the impact depends on music: "The emotional basis of *Cavalcade* was undoubtedly music. The whole story was threaded onto
a string of popular melodies. This ultimately was a big contributing factor to its success. Popular tunes probe the memory more
swiftly than anything else." [12] There was also Coward's original

music, especially the music for *Mirabelle* (Coward's version of
the popular operetta) and the "Twentieth-Century Blues" for the
final night-club scene.

Other devices, many drawn from the films, were used successfully. In the course of many scenes and frequently in the darkness
between them, voices of newsboys shouted headlines. Over the
proscenium, the date of each scene appeared in lights. There were
also a number of scenes which depended on a combination of
visual effects and sounds, but had little or no dialogue. Part I,
Scene 6 is in Kensington Gardens, January 27, 1901; there is no
dialogue: "everyone is in black and they walk slowly as though
perpetually conscious of the country's mourning. Even the children are in black and one woman leading a large brown dog has
tied an enormous black crepe bow on to his collar." Part II,
Scene 7, one of the most effective in production, follows in its
entirety:

Above the proscenium 1914 glows in lights. It changes to 1915, 1916,
1917 and 1918. Meanwhile, soldiers march uphill endlessly. Out of
darkness into darkness. Sometimes they sing gay songs, sometimes they
whistle, sometimes they march silently, but the sound of their tramping
feet is unceasing. Below the vision of them brightly-dressed, energetic
women appear in pools of light, singing stirring recruiting songs—
"Sunday I walk out with a soldier," "We don't want to lose you," etc.,
etc. With 1918 they fade away, as also does the vision of the soldiers,
although the soldiers can still be heard far off, marching and singing
their songs.

Clearly, then, *Cavalcade* is a spectacle of which the sense can
only partially be recaptured by reading the text or by looking at
pictures of the production. *Cavalcade* was in part an attempt to
adapt cinematic techniques to the stage, and it was certainly one
of the last attempts to compete with the camera on these grounds.
Now that the films have proved, even in the case of *Cavalcade*
itself, that they can do such things much better, it is doubtful
whether the play could ever again be produced on stage. Not
even Coward's most elaborate revues and operettes can compare
in complexity.

Nonetheless, the text has a great deal of interest. Some of the
bitterness of *Post-Mortem* finds its way into the play, albeit in a
muted form. Jane Marryot, like John Cavan's mother, represents

the strongest anti-war position, and one of her speeches (when the beginning of World War I is announced) echoes the sentiments of the earlier play: "Drink to the war, then, if you want to. I'm not going to. I can't! Rule Britannia! Send us victorious, happy and glorious! Drink, Joey, you're only a baby, still, but you're old enough for war. Drink like the Germans are drinking, to Victory and Defeat, and stupid, tragic sorrow. But leave me out of it, please!" Furthermore, the last scene, "Evening—1930," begins with Fanny's singing the "Twentieth-Century Blues," a song of disillusion, boredom and near-despair;

When the song is finished, people rise from table and dance without apparently any particular enjoyment; it is the dull dancing of habit. The lights fade away from everything but the dancers, who appear to be rising in the air. They disappear and down stage left six "incurables" in blue hospital uniform are sitting making baskets. They disappear and Fanny is seen singing her song for a moment, then far away up stage a jazz band is seen playing wildly. Then down stage Jane and Robert standing with glasses of champagne held aloft, then Ellen sitting in front of a radio loud speaker; then Margaret dancing with a young man. The visions are repeated quicker and quicker, while across the darkness runs a Riley light sign spelling out news. Noise grows louder and louder. Steam rivets, loud speakers, jazz bands, aeroplane propellers, etc., until the general effect is complete chaos.

Neither attitude is, however, left to remain as a final statement. Jane's earlier bitterness is balanced by her toast of New Year's Eve, 1929, a toast which became the best-remembered and most honored speech in the play: "Now, then, let's couple the Future of England with the past of England. The glories and victories and triumphs that are over, and the sorrows that are over, too. Let's drink to our sons who made part of the pattern and to our hearts that died with them. Let's drink to the spirit of gallantry and courage, that made a strange heaven out of unbelievable Hell, and let's drink to the hope that one day this country of ours, which we love so much, will find dignity and greatness and peace again."

As for the final scene, after achieving chaos, "Suddenly it all fades into darkness and silence and away at the back a Union Jack glows through the blackness. The lights slowly come up and the whole stage is composed of massive tiers, upon which stand the entire Company. The Union Jack flies over their heads as they sing 'God Save the King.'"

When Coward appeared for the curtain speech he says, "It was one of the few occasions of my life that I have ever walked on to a stage not knowing what I was going to say." He delivered "a rather incoherent little speech which finished with the phrase: 'I hope that this play has made you feel that, in spite of the troublous time we are living in, it is still pretty exciting to be English.'" [13] It was certainly a most appropriate curtain line, and a good deal truer to Coward's usual feelings than the despair of *Post-Mortem*.

Cavalcade, a theatrical triumph on a large scale, dazzlingly displayed all of Coward's theatrical talents except his acting, and demonstrated his command of the whole range of popular theater. Examination of one scene, that of Queen Victoria's funeral, reveals how very adept Coward had become. The scene is set in the Marryot drawing-room, a large room with two small balconies overlooking the street. The scene begins quietly and domestically with Jane's serving cocoa and trying to keep the children in line. At first, references to the Queen are muted. Then the cortege is sighted, and the servants are called in. The Marryots and their guests stand on one balcony; the servants, on another. Joe must be reprimanded for throwing cake, Jane worries about Bridges' catching cold, but finally there is silence for a moment. As the music of the death march nears, the children grow more excited and must again be reminded to stand at attention. Persons in the cortege are pointed out. Then, again, there are no words, as everyone stands stiffly; and the music is at its loudest. When the music begins to die away, Cook bursts into tears; and then only two lines are spoken before the lights fade:

Jane: Five kings riding behind her.
Joe: Mum, she must have been a very little lady.

The scene is a model of economy and interwoven themes. There is the grief of the adults counterpointed against the innocent exuberance of the children. However, even the children begin to comprehend; Joe's last line is a masterpiece of sentimental compression and still has the power to moisten eyes when the scene is done as a one-act sketch. There is the sense of ordinary life going forward in a well-to-do but in no way extraordinary household against a background of national mourning which affects all. All is beautifully calculated, balanced and smooth.

If the play seems trite and obvious today, much of that is no doubt due to its very success and to the pattern it helped to set: as a sentimental chronicle, it antedates such works as Laurence Housman's *Victoria Regina* (1935), Marcel Achard's *Auprès de ma blonde* (1945; adapted by S. N. Behrman in 1949 as *I Know My Love*), Jan de Hartog's *The Four-Poster* (1951), and countless films. Coward himself was to return to a variant of the form in *This Happy Breed*, both as a play and a film.

VII   Point Valaine

In typical Coward fashion, *Cavalcade* was followed by *Words and Music*, a work of quite a different type, and one of his most successful revues. This was followed in turn by *Design for Living*, in which the Lunts as actors, and Coward as both writer and actor, displayed their skill in a high comedy. Then came *Conversation Piece*, "a romantic comedy with music," set in Brighton in 1811, in which Coward played a French aristocrat. As if this were not enough variety, and as if he were anxious to repay the Lunts by providing them with a piece that would demonstrate their versatility, Coward wrote *Point Valaine* (1935).

The play is dedicated to William Somerset Maugham, and so it should be. It takes place in Maugham country, a small, semi-tropical island, during the rainy season; the specific locale is a hotel that was once a mission building. The emotional climate is as overheated as the geographical one; and, as if to make the dedication doubly appropriate, Coward has clearly used Maugham as the model for one of his characters. Mortimer Quinn is a novelist who has come to Point Valaine to rest and, if inspiration strikes him, to write; a character of cool detachment, Quinn says of himself: "I always affect to despise human nature. My role in life is clearly marked. Cynical, detached, unscrupulous, an ironic observer and recorder of other people's passions. It is a nice facade to sit behind, but a little bleak."

As a result, he can comment on the action dispassionately and wittily; but, when it serves the plot, he can be marvelously understanding or even sinister. He is also useful for handling the pointer to indicate the tone of the drama: "I prefer more subtle drama, strange little twists in psychology—small unaccountable happenings in people's minds." And twists in psychology are the focus. Linda Valaine, in her early forties, owns the hotel. Helping Linda run the hotel is Stefan, a Russian refugee, a brutish, brooding man. A new guest is Martin Welford, a young pilot who is taking a rest cure after two harrowing weeks in the jungle following a plane crash. Martin and Linda are drawn together, although the audience learns fairly early that Linda is Stefan's mistress. Finally, on a night when Stefan is stranded on a neighboring island because the launch is out of commission, Linda allows Martin to come to her room. Stefan manages to get back, discovers what is happening; hysterically plays his accordion outside Linda's door; and, when she comes out, viciously and loudly sneers at her present lover. After Martin leaves, Stefan becomes abject; he pleads with Linda to remain true to him. She refuses and tells Stefan that she wishes he were dead. In despair, Stefan leaps into the sea. The next morning one of the servants discovers Stefan's shark-torn body at the shore. Linda can only say, in a harsh, cold voice: "I must see about engaging a new head waiter."

The play was unsuccessful both in England and in America. Coward attributed this to the weakness of theme and character: "It was neither big enough for tragedy nor light enough for comedy; the characters were well drawn, but not one of them was either interesting or kind. The young man, the only one with any claim to sympathy from the audience . . . struck me on closer analysis as silly, overidealistic, and a prig." [14]

The characters are interesting enough to support the needs of a melodrama, which is all the play can claim to be; but, even as such, it fails most seriously. The trouble lies in the slow tempo of the play, particularly the first two acts, and in the sporadic and somewhat artificial manner in which the plot emerges. Furthermore, the peripheral material—comic pictures of vacationers, Quinn's problems with a young magazine writer, details of hotel management—is by no means as amusing as it is meant to be and is constantly interfering with the main tale. Act I is almost pure exposition of an extremely mechanical type. The scene of Stefan's rage, which begins Act III, is by far the best scene in the play and is one of Coward's rare and most successful attempts at putting raw feelings on the stage. However, by then it is too late to save the play which has been waiting desperately for this moment.

Coward has often built a successful three-act play out of material that might seem thin for a fifteen-minute sketch—*Private Lives* is the best example—yet in *Point Valaine,* where the basic outline is more than adequate for a full-length work, much of the play is padding. As it happens, Coward's next venture was into the realm of the one-act play where he was to be far more successful in dealing with "twists in psychology—small unaccountable happenings in people's minds."

VIII *One Acts*

For that delightful and eminently successful potpourri entitled *Tonight at 8:30,* Coward provided two serious plays, *The Astonished Heart* and *Still Life,* both of which are among the best things he has done. Perhaps, as Terence Rattigan remarks, "it is difficult . . . for him to sustain a serious mood for long." [15]

The title of *The Astonished Heart* is explained in the play itself when Christian Faber, the protagonist, decides to check a biblical quotation for a speech he is preparing. The quotation, Deuteronomy xxviii, 28, states that, as a punishment for disobedience, "The Lord shall smite thee with madness, and blindness, and astonishment of the heart." Such is the fate of Faber, although the madness and blindness are metaphorical. An eminent psychiatrist, Faber finds himself suddenly "submerged" in a passionate affair with Leonora Vail, a former schoolmate of his wife Barbara. Barbara recommends that Christian and Leonora enjoy an extended holiday until passion cools and Christian is able to return to his wife and his work with a clear head; but her remedy fails. While Leonora's ardor wanes, Christian grows even more irrational, jealousy now adding to his frenzy. Finally, Leonora breaks the bond; and Christian throws himself from the window. On his deathbed, he calls for Leonora; but after she sees him, moments before his death, she can only report, "He didn't know me, he thought I was you, he said—'Baba—I'm not submerged any more'—and then he said 'Baba' again—and then—then he died."

Perhaps largely because of the compression of the one-act play, *The Astonished Heart* is one of Coward's most successful serious works. The characteristically too-easily-defined personality, who is so frequent in many of Coward's plays, would in any case be more readily acceptable in a play lasting less than hour, but Christian and Barbara Faber are actually better developed than Lucy in *Sirocco*. Christian's three scenes of progressively greater irrationality are concisely yet convincingly done, and there is no sense of the arbitrary or of the manipulated in his suicide. Barbara is even better done; her strength, her common sense and her poise are solid. In the scene in which she suggests that her husband and his mistress take a holiday together, no readjustment of perceptions is needed. Of the three main characters, only Leonora remains somewhat ill-defined. Is she really not much more than a philanderess, or was she serious before Christian's jealousy destroyed their love? The mystery is not, however, terribly important since she does not occupy the center of attention for any great length of time.

When *The Astonished Heart* was first performed in London, Ivor Brown found the acting unsatisfactory: "Mr. Coward and Miss Lawrence play the desperate lovers in the tight-lipped, back-to-the-audience, self-suppressive, word-swallowing style of emotional acting which is fashionable today. Of this style they offer a first-rate example, but it is not a good style of acting for a play the paramount interest of which lies in the violence of erotic passion and in the virtuosity with which this demonic possession is portrayed. I should define *The Astonished Heart* as a piece for 'ham' actors presented by vegetarians of the first lustre." [16]

Although Mr. Brown surely underestimated the amount of self-suppressive behavior inherent in the play, his comment is a valuable one. Not only does it provide a concise picture of Coward as an actor in serious roles, but it points to a basic weakness in Coward's whole treatment of serious situations. In many of Coward's plays the most promising scenes—in the sense of being emotionally climactic—are weakened by the characters' tendency to analyze and summarize rather than to explode in a truly passionate manner. The last scenes of *The Vortex* and of *Sirocco* are particularly weak. Christian Faber's speeches indicate how far Coward had come in refining, but not actually overcoming this characteristic procedure; and Brown's comment calls attention to the way this approach is underlined in production. Again the one-act structure, with its insistent demand for compression, is a decisive factor; developed as a full-length play, *The Astonished Heart* would hardly have been as successful if the level of emotional expression had remained the same.

It is more than the one-act form that creates success in *Still*

Life. In it, the setting and circumstances not only compel just such tight-lipped utterance but also create a sense of explosive emotions in the very process of negating any opportunity for them to be vented. *Still Life* is, like *The Astonished Heart*, a multi-scened play tracing the course of illicit love from beginning to end. The setting throughout is the refreshment room of the Milford Junction railroad station. In the background are some railway employees. Mrs. Bagot, manager of the refreshment room and a very "refined" widow, is being jocularly courted by Albert Godby, a ticket inspector. Mrs. Bagot's assistant, Beryl Waters, a young girl, is much admired by Stanley, a candy butcher. This group forms a comic genre picture that is almost a play in itself. In the foreground are Alec Harvey and Laura Jesson. He is a general practitioner who comes into Milford once a week to work at the hospital on his special interest, preventive medicine. She is a housewife who comes in almost every week for shopping and a movie. The play follows the course of their romance from an accidental meeting, when Alec takes a cinder out of Laura's eye, to their parting.

The crisis in the relationship occurs when Laura finally agrees to meet Alec at the apartment of a friend who is always out until late. On this day, unfortunately, the friend returns early and discovers the lovers. Terribly humiliated, Laura decides that they must stop seeing each other; reluctantly Alec agrees and decides to accept a job in public health in Johannesburg. Their last meeting, some weeks later, is interrupted by Dolly Messiter, one of Laura's friends, who joins the two at their table and gossips until Alec has left for his train. Laura rushes out to the platform—she may be contemplating suicide—but then returns; and the play ends.

Coward thought *Still Life* the "most mature play" of all the more or less serious plays in *Tonight at 8:30*. Its maturity is one both of form and content. The counterpoint between foreground and background is brilliantly done. In almost every way the story of Mrs. Bagot and her circle contributes directly to the total effect. First, the realistic setting, with its stir of activity, underlines the painful control needed by the two protagonists, as well as their isolation. Second, Mrs. Bagot's scolding, nagging, and general uppishness are both funny in themselves (her concern about the symmetry of her arrangement of cakes is a good example); and these characteristics make an ironic contrast to the concealment, the furtiveness and, most of all, the deep passion of Alec and Laura. There is a sense of class distinction here, for middle-class nuances of feeling contrast with the coarser, more superficial responses of the Cockney; but diversity is only stressed enough to throw the central story into higher relief.

In addition, there are the changes in the relationships between Mrs. Bagot and Albert and between Beryl and Stanley that show how time is passing and how these people are free to delay and skirmish, to marry, and to play at courtship almost indefinitely. However, none of this contrast is stressed. On the contrary, the total effect is that of the thoroughly achieved realistic play, where nothing seems planned but all is natural, fluid, almost accidental. The same quality appears in the dialogues between Alec and Laura. Coward presents the fragments of a continuing conversation, but we are always informed of what is happening. We are able to pick up immediately the story line and the emotional tone in each scene despite the fact that Alec's and Laura's appearances in the room are only the tag ends of the days they spend together.

So successful is the whole presentation that it comes as a surprise to realize how very slight the story itself is. The three major steps in the plot—the cinder in the eye, the apartment owner's unexpected return, and the gossipy friend's frustration of the final meeting—are well-worn coincidences. The theme that basic decency wins out is hardly a novel idea. Yet, both characters and their situation are endowed with a weight and substance that are rare for Coward. In large part the solidity of the refreshment room gives such reality to the lovers, but they are also very carefully observed individuals. Finally, and perhaps most significantly, the whole play is given life and its fullest pathos by the restrained dialogue, in which little is said but much implied.

Excellent proof of the value of the form of *Still Life* can be found in the film version that Coward wrote, *Brief Encounter*. Although he needed to expand the story considerably in order to make a full-length film, and although he introduced a wide range of locales to supplement the railroad refreshment room, Coward wisely adhered to the same basic pattern: the fragile love of Laura and Alec constantly hampered and always threatened by the essentially public nature of their meetings.

IX This Happy Breed

Coward's fullest examination of the simple annals of simple people was his next serious play, *This Happy Breed,* written in 1939 but not produced until late in 1942. Although Coward refers to the play as "a suburban middle-class family comedy," it surely belongs in this chapter rather than the next. It does have a happy ending, a good many comic moments, and few moments of pathos or pain. The over-all tone, however, is one of gentle reminiscence; and the mood at the end of the play is quiet, even meditative.

Covering the period between June, 1919, to June, 1939, *This Happy Breed* chronicles the life of the Gibbons family from the time they move into a house at No. 17 Sycamore Road, Clapham Common, to the day they move out. The play begins as Frank Gibbons, recently demobilized from the army, moves into No. 17 with his family: his wife, Ethel; his sister, Sylvia; his mother-in-law, Mrs. Flint; and three children, Vi, Queenie, and Reg. On the first day, they discover that their next-door neighbors are the Mitchells; Bob Mitchell and Frank Gibbons had known each other in the army. In this first scene most of the thematic lines are established. Mrs. Flint and Sylvia are eternally quarreling. Ethel and Frank are very much in love, but of rather different natures: she is religious, prudish and conventional, even slightly shrewish; he is agnostic, tolerant and sensible. How they will all act in a crisis is predictable, but this is no weakness, suspense not being a major ingredient of the play. Indeed, the plot is essentially unsensational. Reg comes under the influence of Sam Leadbitter, a Communist, and has a falling out with the family during the General Strike of 1926. Soon afterwards, however, both give up their radicalism; Sam marries Vi Gibbons and settles down, and Reg marries Phyllis Blake, a girl very much like his sister Vi. Less than a year later, both Reg and Phyllis are killed in an automobile accident.

The most important dramatic focus of the play is Queenie. Although in love with Billy Mitchell, Queenie resents the limitations of middle-class life and runs away with a married man. Frank is sympathetic and would like to keep track of his daughter, but Ethel tries her best to forget Queenie and will not have her name mentioned in the house. Five years later, Billy returns home on leave from the navy married to Queenie. He has found her in

France where she has spent the last four years at various jobs since being deserted by her lover. After only a moment's hesitation, Ethel welcomes her back. The play ends a few years later: Queenie has gone to Singapore to join Billy, leaving her child in her parents' charge. Bob Mitchell, whose wife had died a few years before, has moved out of the house next door; Sam and Vi are busy with their children; Mrs. Flint is dead; and Sylvia has become Mrs. Wilmot's assistant at the Christian Science "reading and rest room in Baker Street." Frank and·Ethel are preparing to move out of No. 17 into a small flat where Frank will learn to do without a garden and a cat. As Ethel works in another room, Frank talks to Queenie's baby. It is June, 1939:

There's not much to worry about really, so long as you remember one or two things always. The first is that life isn't all jam for anybody, and you've got to have trouble of some kind or another, whoever you are. But if you don't let it get you down, however bad it is, you won't go far wrong. . . . We're human beings, we are—all of us—and that's what people are liable to forget. Human beings don't like peace and good will and everybody loving everybody else. However much they may think they do, they don't because they're not made like that. Human beings like eating and drinking and loving and hating. They also like showing off, grabbing all they can, fighting for their rights, and bossing anybody who'll give 'em half a chance. You belong to a race that's been bossy for years and the reason it's held on as long as it has is that nine times out of ten it's behaved decently and treated people right. Just lately, I'll admit, we've been giving at the knees a bit and letting people down who trusted us and allowing noisy little men to bully us with a lot of guns and bombs and aeroplanes. But don't worry—that won't last—the people themselves, the ordinary people like you and me know something better than all the fussy old politicians put together—we know what we belong to, where we come from, and where we're going. We may not know it with our brains, but we know it with our roots. And we know another thing, too, and it's this. We 'aven't lived and died and struggled all these hundreds of years to get decency and justice and freedom for ourselves without being prepared to fight fifty wars if need be—to keep 'em.

The play is a sort of *Cavalcade* seen through the wrong end of the telescope: instead of epic or pageant, there are nine scenes all set in the Gibbons' dining room; instead of hundreds, a cast of twelve; instead of wars, royal balls and royal funerals, the General

Strike, the abdication of Edward VIII, and Chamberlain's visit to
Munich. Even these matters are pushed into the background, the
concern being much more with a realistic picture of family
change. Only the faith in English staunchness has remained un-
dimmed since Coward's curtain speech for *Cavalcade*.

The difference between *Cavalcade* and *This Happy Breed* reflects a real and profound change in English life. Although written
less than ten years earlier, *Cavalcade* has a basically aristocratic
outlook. The Marryots are members of the ruling class while the
Bridges are servants and pubkeepers, and between them stretches
a void. There are indications toward the end of the play that this
situation is changing, but these indications are brief and almost
perfunctory. The focus in *Cavalcade* is always on Jane Marryot, a
lady in far more than name. A tribute to England and English
virtues, *Cavalcade* is a far cry from *This Happy Breed,* Coward's
tribute to the ordinary Englishman. The imminence of war hangs
over the play, and it is the middle-class soldier, sailor, and civilian
whom Coward recognizes now as the object of concern. Alfred
Bridges went proudly off to the Boer War as Robert Marryot's bat
man, the master-servant relationship undisturbed; but forty years
later, Frank Gibbons, who could well be Alfred Bridges' son,
would hardly see himself or his children in such a position.

The work as a whole does not contain much obvious patriotic
appeal, or much preaching of any sort. Its real strength lies, as
with *Still Life,* in the solidity and weight of the characters, no
matter how trivial the moment. As might be expected, the comic
moments are major contributions to the play's success, and Mrs.
Flint and Sylvia, as Dickensian a pair of characters as Coward
ever drew, carry most of the comic burden.

The body of the play consists of genre pictures. There is, naturally enough with the dining-room setting, much serving of tea
and meals. There the family gathers around the radio listening to
the abdication speech. There is a Christmas party; some mild ca-
rousing when Frank and Bob Mitchell return drunk from a gathering of veterans; and, at the beginning and the end of the play,
scenes of moving—boxes and hampers, pictures off the walls, bare
windows. In its less spectacular way, *This Happy Breed* depends
almost as much on visual effects as does *Cavalcade;* for, unless the
realistic passage of time can be convincingly presented, all else
fails.

X Peace In Our Time

This Happy Breed, completed just before the outbreak of World War II, is one 'of Coward's gentlest plays; *Peace In Our Time,* written in 1947, is the most violent and melodramatic. *This Happy Breed* celebrates the English doggedness which Coward hoped would see England through the worst that might come. *Peace In Our Time* pictures the English undergoing the very worst: occupation by the Germans. The stimulus for the play came from Coward's visit to Paris soon after the Liberation:

Almost immediately upon my arrival in Paris I found myself in a delicate and embarrassing position regarding many of my French theatrical colleagues. There was unease and tension in the atmosphere and a great deal of gossip and argument on all sides about who had collaborated and who hadn't; who had been passive; who had been active; who had been concerned with the Resistance; who had been moderate; who had been pro-British and who had been anti, etc. . . .

A little later, when I returned to England, I started a private game with a few of my intimate friends. This game was a hypothetical discussion of what would have happened to the English theatre and our associates in it if, in the autumn of 1940, the Battle of Britain had been lost instead of won and our country had been invaded and occupied by the Germans. It was a cruel little game . . . but it did serve a purpose because it gave me the idea of writing a play about the occupation of England. I chose the setting of a London public house because it seemed to me that only in such a deep-rooted institution as a British "pub" could I assemble together enough varied and representative types to illustrate my theme.[17]

As proprietor of the pub "The Shy Gazelle," Coward used Fred Shattuck, very much the same solid, sensible and profoundly, if quietly, patriotic Englishman as Frank Gibbons.

Peace In Our Time takes its title from Prime Minister Chamberlain's statement of reassurance upon his return, in 1938, from signing the Munich Pact—the one which opened the door for Hitler's takeover of Czechoslovakia. This phrase grew ever more infamous as World War II ran its ugly course, and its use as a title for a play dealing with an England in defeat, a fate which Chamberlain's policies brought close to reality, was a brilliant one.

The play is in two acts of four scenes each. The first scene is in

November, 1940, shortly after the Germans have occupied England; the last takes place in May, 1945, as the Resistance comes to full life with the Allied armies approaching London. In the other scenes the course of the Occupation is traced. At first resentful but unsure, most of the English gradually become involved in underground activities; some continue with their regular lives, like Phyllis, the barmaid, whose chief interest is the cinema; and a few, especially Gladys Mott, a prostitute, and Chorley Bannister, editor of an intellectual magazine, become collaborators.

At first, the Germans are confident that the sensible English will succumb to the "Inevitable," but slowly the invaders become oppressive. The climax is Doris Shattuck's death after torture. The final scene provides an emotional catharsis. As the street-fighting grows more intense, George Bourne brings to The Shy Gazelle a Nazi functionary, Albrecht Richter. The Resistance forces are going to kill him in retaliation for Doris's death, but they decide to let the German troops do the job for them. They tie him to a chair, gag him, face him toward the locked door, put a Resistance armband on his arm and a Resistance cap over his face, turn on the forbidden radio station, and leave by the back door. A moment later, the Germans arrive; and, finding the door locked, they fire round after round of machine gun bullets through the door. Richter topples to the floor as the curtain falls.

The methods of *Still Life* and of *This Happy Breed* are applied once more with great success. The setting, simple and ordinary, provides a strong counterpoint between the unsensational and unheroic setting and actions on stage and the violent, dangerous, and heroic actions which occur mainly off stage. The importance of the solidly realistic picture to be created on-stage is indicated in Coward's remarks on the difficulty of producing the play in America:

In the English production we rehearsed from the first day in the actual set. The bar and the bar stools, the glasses, bottles, cigarettes, ash trays, etc. were all in place so that the actors, by the time we reached our opening night . . . knew exactly how to co-ordinate their dialogue with their props and business.

In the American theatre this kind of production would be out of the question. . . . None of the actual furniture or properties can be used without the employment of a full staff, and the cost of this would naturally be so crippling to a production that no management could be expected to pay it.[18]

In addition to the setting, the major factors contributing to the realistic effect are the characters and the construction of the episodes. The location of the pub, "somewhere between Knightsbridge and Sloane Square," allows for a vivid assortment of customers ranging from some theater people, like Lyia Vivian, and writers, like Chorley Bannister and Janet Braid, to some rather ordinary folk, nondescript like the Graingers or drunkenly argumentative like the Blakes. None, however, is terribly important in public life as far as the usual hierarchies of importance are concerned, although late in the play George Bourne does turn out to be "the Boss" of the Resistance. Much the same is true of the enemy; aside from occasional soldiers who appear to check identification cards or come with Gladys Mott, the only Nazi is Richter, a sincere adherent to his country's policies and goals, but not a particularly important member of the German forces. The stress is, therefore, on the routine rather than the unusual; the Resistance activities themselves enter the picture gradually, almost automatically, paralleling as it were the decline in both the quantity and the quality of the spirits available at the bar.

Each scene follows a basic pattern. Beginning with a loose and apparently undynamic picture of the saloon bar with an assorted group of characters talking in random fashion, each gradually grows to some sort of climax which adds to the developing plot and tension. This basic method of *Still Life* and of *This Happy Breed* was first developed by Coward in some of the key scenes of *Cavalcade*.

The first scene of *Peace In Our Time* establishes the pattern. The regulars in the bar talk together, asking about trips they have taken, word from their families, etc. There are some oblique and caustic references to "them," otherwise not identified. About halfway through the scene, Janet Braid and Chorley Bannister begin to argue about Bannister's editorial adaptability, but on the surface there is no particular reason to interpret this in political terms. Shortly thereafter, when Richter enters, all conversation stops when he buys a drink. He tries, not very successfully, to make conversation, then leaves. Still, nothing is clear, though the air has grown thicker and more ominous. Richter's nationality is not discussed—he speaks English perfectly—and although his appearance adds new fuel to the quarrel between Chorley and Janet, the lines of disagreement remain abstract.

Then, Nora Shattuck turns on the radio to get the news. The announcer is a standard British Broadcasting Company type and he gives some ambiguous war news before discussing plans for the next day's opening of Parliament. There is nothing particularly unusual about these plans until the last seconds of the scene when the announcer presents the order of the procession: "In the first open landau will be seated the Fuehrer. The carriages following will contain Air Chief Marshal Goering, Dr. Goebbels, and high-ranking Army, Navy and Air Force officers. . . ." And *"The lights fade."* No other scene attempts quite so shattering a surprise, but the outline remains the same for the rest of the play. Even in that last scene, with the sound of grenades and guns in the background, the opening minutes still have an air of nonchalance.

In the foreword to the American edition, Coward attempts to forestall criticism of the play's "unabashed patriotism" by asking his readers to imagine how they might feel were America in the same situation. In truth, the patriotism of *Peace In Our Time* is much more penetrating than that in *Cavalcade* or *This Happy Breed*. Not only do the circumstances of the play do much to justify the patriotic appeals, but Coward has succeeded in making his tirades dramatically dynamic. Janet Braid, witty and articulate, lashing out at Bannister, sets the adrenalin flowing in both actress and audience:

As these are the last words I ever intend to address to you, Chorley, I want you to remember them. First of all, I despise you from the bottom of my soul. You and your kind pride yourselves on being intellectuals, don't you? You babble a lot of snobbish nonsense about art and letters and beauty. You consider yourselves to be far above such primitive emotions as love and hate and devotion to a cause. You run your little high-brow magazines and change your politics with every wind that blows. . . . In the years before the war you were squealing for disarmament at a moment when to be fully armed was vitally necessary for our survival. You were all pacifists then. . . . Later, a very little later, having listened obediently to a few foreign agitators, you were launching virulent attacks on British imperialism. That was when you were all bright little Communists. Now of course your intellectual ardours are devoted exclusively to Fascism—an easy transition. Where are you going next—you clever ones? What will your attitude be when England is free again, when your German friends are blasted to hell and driven into oblivion? You had better make your plans quickly— there is hardly any time to be lost. Get ready for a lightning change of views, Chorley. Make it snappy, you drivelling little rat. . . . And when you are arranging with your friends to have me put into a con- centration camp, remember to tell them exactly what I said. I said, "Down with Hitler!" And I hope he rots in hell with all the strutting, yelping jackals round him! Down with the Third Bloody Reich and down into the lowest depths with every Englishman who gave our enemies lip service and fawned on them and by so doing flung his country's pride into the dust!

[*Janet gives Chorley two ringing slaps on the face which send him staggering against the bar, and walks out.*]

Oversimplified, sophomoric, melodramatic? Of course. But how very satisfying this speech is because it comes when it does.

XI Waiting in the Wings

In *Still Life, This Happy Breed,* and *Peace In Our Time,* Cow- ard achieved great poignancy and force by embedding each firmly in a matrix of scrupulously observed and vividly and wittily presented routine life. Even the melodrama of *Peace In Our Time* is familiar enough, and the fact that this action occurs in Eng- land would be at best only an ingenious variation on a standard pattern without the solidity of The Shy Gazelle. In each case, the background has served to heighten the force of the story by un- derlining its verisimilitude and by providing a channel for Cow- ard's powers of restrained understatement. Furthermore, in each case the setting and background have their own interest in the details of ordinary life. In Coward's *Waiting in the Wings* (1960), this method has been carried one step farther, for in this play setting and background are virtually all there is since the story hardly exists.

Waiting in the Wings is set in a "small charity home for retired actresses." Those who live there have all been leading ladies; none is under sixty, and all are very much aware that they have little to look forward to except death. The play is held together by a few

unifying strands: the problem of getting the Committee to build a
solarium; the problem of reconciling May Davenport and Lotta
Bainbridge, who are now daily confronted with each other after
thirty years of enmity; the problem of Sarita Myrtle, who grows
more and more senile and loves to play with matches. A newspaper's article on The Wings (the name of the home) results, after
considerable squabbling and difficulties, in the publisher's providing the money for the solarium; at the end of the play the old
ladies who most bitterly complained of the cold wind on the ter-
race are beginning to complain that the solarium is too hot, a typically Cowardian touch of ironic symmetry. May and Lotta are
reconciled on the night Sarita sets fire to the curtains in her room.
Sarita is taken away to an asylum, but makes a superb exit.

In addition, Deirdre O'Malley, sharp-tongued and over-pious,
dies of a heart-attack. Lotta receives a visit from her son, who had
gone to Canada thirty-three years before with her husband and
from whom she had heard almost nothing since. She gently and
painfully refuses to go to live with him and his family. Perry Las-
coe, secretary to the Committee and much beloved by all the ladies, is fired for his part in arranging for a reporter to visit The
Wings; he is reinstated thanks to May's influence. Osgood Meeker,
aged seventy continues to come every Sunday to visit Martha
Carrington, aged ninety-five, with whom he has been in love since
he was seventeen. And Miss Archie, the resident superintendent,
continues to cope in her military way. All of this activity is of
importance or interest only insofar as it provides opportunities for
observing the ladies in action.

Such a structure allows not only for a large number of elderly
actresses to demonstrate their versatility, but for Coward to demonstrate his as well. Here his interest in and his nostalgia for the
old songs and old musical shows are seen. The ladies often reminisce about their early years, and sing some of the old songs; and
the play ends with almost everybody on stage singing "Oh Mr.
Kaiser" to welcome a new arrival, Topsy Baskerville, who had
once made the song famous. Coward's talent for writing scenes of
restrained pathos is shown particularly in Lotta's meeting with
her son. Of character comedy, there is Deirdre O'Malley. Of
wild, fantastic comedy, we have Sarita's ramblings, mingling
lines from old plays, backstage jargon, details of her past life
and occasional moments of clarity. The witty, slightly bad-

tempered badinage of the characteristic Coward type is present throughout, but appears particularly in the scenes involving Lotta and May.

Despite its versatility and other charms, *Waiting in the Wings* is not a success. A meaningful sense of loss, of waste, of imminent death does not develop, although Coward is careful to have these themes frequently mentioned. Not only the retired ladies but even the younger people involved are all such "characters" that they can only sporadically engage the audience's sympathies. Of the three crucial moments of the play, only Lotta's dismissal of her son really carries much weight. Deirdre's death and Sarita's departure for the asylum are ironic and striking but they remain theatrical clichés—they do not touch the audience.

XII Suite in Three Keys

First produced in London in April and May of 1966, *Suite in Three Keys* consists of three works: *A Song at Twilight*, a full-length play, and two one-acts, *Shadows of the Evening* and *Come into the Garden Maud*. The first two are serious plays, the last a light comedy. All three use the same setting, a hotel suite in a Swiss hotel. The central figure in each play is an elderly man—in *A Song at Twilight*, a novelist in many ways similar to Somerset Maugham; in *Come into the Garden Maud*, an American millionaire; and in *Shadows of the Evening*, a publisher—and in each play he is in conflict with his wife and mistress. All three plays are, like *Waiting in the Wings* and some of Coward's most recent fiction, preoccupied with age, illness, and death; and they end with a reassertion of love and stoic agnosticism.

These three plays provided another demonstration of Coward's versatility both as an author and an actor (he played all three leading male roles), but they are little more than mechanically skillful reworkings of familiar material. In *Come into the Garden Maud*, a good-hearted, henpecked American leaves his social-climbing wife for a warm hearted woman of the world. In *Shadows of the Evening*, after the doctor diagnoses the hero's illness as incurable, husband, wife and mistress agree to live as happily and fully as possible for the few remaining months. *A Song at Twilight* has slightly more substance, and caused a brief stir in London because in it the author argued against the British law making homosexual acts a crime. However, the law was already being

rewritten at the time the play was produced, and Coward's frankness and outrage, limited to this single legal problem in an otherwise thin and predictable story, are already out of date.

XIII   Coward's Development

Terence Rattigan has aptly stated that "development" is too
often taken to mean attempting more and more serious subjects,
or striving to emulate some critic's standard that may have little to
do with the writer's interests and abilities. Coward, he says, developed as "we all develop . . . by the simple process of growing
and gathering experience," and by improving his craft.[19] By setting *Waiting in the Wings* next to *The Vortex* we may indicate
how accurate this statement is. The subject matter of *The Vortex*
is, if anything, more serious, and certainly more sensational and
more forcefully presented; but how much better the playwright
knows and understands the ladies of The Wings.

Coward's serious plays show, therefore, a clear line of change,
one moving from harrowing and lurid subjects—dope addiction,
gigoloism, and torrid seduction—to more ordinary topics—old
age, family loyalty and bereavement—and from exotic characters
and settings more and more into the boundaries of middle-class
life. The alarms and excursions of *Peace In Our Time* are in the
long run only temporary, if painful, interruptions in the even and
healthy tenor of solid English life; and in *Waiting in the Wings* it
is ultimately more important that the characters are old ladies
preparing for death than that they are all former stars.

Coward's development in play construction parallels his
changes in subject matter. The success of *The Vortex* depends in
large part on a sequence of strenuously witty and explosively
emotional scenes tied together any which way, but *Waiting in the
Wings* shows a well-trained and assured, as opposed to a cocksure,
hand at work. We could hardly imagine the twenty-five-year-old
Coward attempting to maintain interest for long without rely-
ing on melodramatic, "strong" situations, complete with applause-
sparking curtain lines.

It would be a mistake, however, to overemphasize differences
while ignoring how the later plays reflect many of the same premises and limitations of the earlier ones. At the heart of almost
every play is the concept of the "whacking good part," although
the stress has changed from ranting to subtle delineation. But,

although an actor's enthusiasm can grow out of an author's profound concern with a character—Shakespeare's Hamlet, for example, or Ibsen's Hedda Gabler—the reverse is rarely, if ever,
true: a playwright's· determination to provide himself or some
other character with a striking part is not enough—and this fault
has generally been Coward's. Frank Gibbons is a far cry from
Nicky Lancaster, but they are brothers under the skin, both collections of bits and pieces, neither a fully created character. Frank
comes closer; it is possible to imagine him in various situations,
but Nicky exists only in the play, perhaps only when an actor
lends him some of his own reality. Even at his most serious, Coward remains a comic writer, one who peoples his plays with basically two-dimensional characters. They are, in the older sense of
the word, "humorous" characters—embodiments of a few distinctive traits.

The level of significance in Coward's serious plays has also not
changed much over the decades. Bothered since the early 1930's
by certain weaknesses in English society, Coward has dramatized
his concerns in a number of plays, primarily in *Post-Mortem, Cavalcade, This Happy Breed,* and *Peace In Our Time;* but the analysis has never penetrated far beyond the level of the popular magazine. Despite the pessimism of *Post-Mortem,* Coward has usually
found solace in the enduring value of sound English character;
and he has defined such value in platitudes. In the plays which are
non-political—*The Astonished Heart, Still Life,* and *Waiting in
the Wings,* for example—the same is true on a psychological level;
there is pathos but not tragedy, and English stoicism is the chief
virtue. This characteristic of the plays is unobjectionable certainly, but thin.

The Vortex may have struck a large part of the audience as a
vehement denunciation of vice and as an exposé of the silver cord
as a garotte. In the early 1930's it may still have seemed reasonable to think of Coward as "fundamentally a Savonarola." [20] In
retrospect, however, it appears that Coward was always more
concerned with theatrical effectiveness than with finding forms
in which to present ideas or denunciations that demanded expression. Such themes as are presented are Coward's reflections
on matters that are in the air; and, while his presentation is usually intelligent and sincere, even briefly startling in novelty or out-
spokenness, it rarely goes beyond the superficial.

In conclusion, to Coward's work in serious dramas (as is true with minor variations about all his work except several of the best comedies) time has brought a considerable increase in skill and some changes in subject matter but little change in the level of perception and significance. As a writer of serious plays, Coward has remained an artist admired for his skill, his sensibleness, and his charm. The serious tone he can best create and maintain is one of a gentle, restrained pathos; but Coward's effects grow far less out of depths of character or a philosophical view of society than from an awareness of theatrical effect. So long as the theater remains wedded to realism, at least some of these works—*Still Life, This Happy Breed,* perhaps even *The Vortex*—are certain to be performed, while others which are less likely to be produced—*Cavalcade, Peace In Our Time,* and *Post-Mortem*—should find readers for some time to come.

CHAPTER 4

Comedy

IN the labelling of his plays, Noel Coward has helped to categorize his work. In musical productions he has been ingenious in distinguishing between different types: *Conversation Piece*, for example, is subtitled *A Romantic Comedy with Music; Bitter-Sweet, An Operette;* and *Pacific 1860, A Musical Romance.* Any theater piece which has a primarily serious intent is called, simply, "A Play." For the comedies, he has remained faithful to two labels, "A Light Comedy" and "A Comedy." Slight as the difference may seem between these two, the names fairly consistently indicate a distinct difference in type: those called "light" are high farces, and those labeled simply "comedies" are in the older tradition of the comedy of manners.

High farce was born full grown in Oscar Wilde's *The Importance of Being Earnest* (1895). This play has frequently been called a combination of farce and high comedy, but such is not its true nature. Combinations have been frequent since the time of Shakespeare—*Much Ado About Nothing* is a good example—but they differ radically from Wilde's play. Even in such an elegant comedy as William Congreve's *The Way of the World,* we find at least two distinct groups of characters (and often distinct plots as well). The one group of characters is composed of the articulate, witty, elegant figures who spring so easily to mind when "high comedy" is mentioned, Beatrice and Benedick, or Mirabell and Millamant, and all those other "witty couples." On the other hand, we have the dolts, the country bumpkins, the clumsy fools who become embroiled in ridiculous misunderstandings and improbable situations. The witty ones, however, are always a group apart; they may become involved in ridiculous situations, they may even help to create them; but they always grasp the difference, are never touched by the slapstick, and at the end are united in sensible matrimony or find themselves in some comparably ra-

tional situation. The fools are either laughed off the stage or un-
mistakably chastised and shown their place.

In *The Importance of Being Earnest* such distinctions between
sense and foolishness are, however, largely lost. All the situations
are ridiculous, but no character stands aloof from them; in fact, all
are deadly serious. Some, of course, are more foolish than others;
but their foolishness is measured, not against the rational and the
sensible but against a standard as artificial and ridiculous as it is
thematically elegant. The worst misreading of Wilde's play is to
call it a "satire." It has satirical statements and some satirical implications, but so does James Barrie's *Peter Pan;* and Wilde's play
and Barrie's have more in common than does *The Importance of
Being Earnest* and, say, *Epicoene.* What Wilde calls "London"
and "Woolton" are his never-never land, and he demands consent
to the existence of this rarefied world as insistently as Peter Pan
demands applause to save Tinkerbell.

I Hay Fever

Coward has never created a high farce as perfect as Wilde's,
but there have been times when he has come very close. The first
time was *Hay Fever*, written in 1924, in which the never-never
land is the "hall of the Blisses' house at Cookham." Judith is an
actress, frequently retired, whose specialty on the stage is portray-
ing long-suffering, noble women. David, her husband, is a popular
novelist whose books have titles like *The Sinful Woman* and
Broken Reeds. There are a daughter, Sorel, and a son, Simon,
both apparently in their late 'teens or early twenties. The rule of
the house is *laissez-faire,* and each member of the family has invited a weekend guest without consulting or even notifying the
others. The play concerns the reception and treatment of the
guests; it ends when the guests make a furtive escape after one
memorable night.

Each guest represents some fantasy on the part of his host. Judith, playing the role of the Celebrated Actress and Temptress
masquerading as Lady of the Manor, invites Sandy Tyrell, a
young, handsome, and unsophisticated boxer who should provide
open-mouthed homage to her grace and glamor. David invites
Jackie Coryton, a naïve young girl whom he intends to study "in
domestic surroundings." Sorel, longing for respectability and conformity, invites Richard Greatham, "a diplomatist." And Simon,

hoping to define and practice his manhood, has invited cool, sophisticated, worldly Myra Arundel. Each Bliss, except David, greets his guest rapturously; but each ignores all the others. The first act ends with the guests thoroughly confused and shaken.

The second act begins with a game which deteriorates into a furious quarrel among the Blisses and results in a reshuffling of partners. Each duo is given its chance on stage, and each scene ends with Judith at the center of a scene of renunciation or of motherly grief. At the peak of the commotion, Richard enters to ask innocently, "Is this a game?" The Blisses, who pick this up as a cue, promptly re-enact the melodramatic finale of Judith's great success, *Love's Whirlwind*. At its climax, Judith swoons, while the guests look on "dazed and aghast."

In the final act, the next morning, the guests decide to leave at once and slip away in Sandy's car. The Blisses react in characteristic fashion.

Judith: How very rude!
David: People really do behave in the most extraordinary manner these days—

And rudeness is the keystone of the play, for it is also the keystone of the Blisses' lives, despite their sporadic attempts to reform and to behave sensibly. They are not consciously rude, but are so well attuned to each other's thoughts and feelings that they rarely find it necessary to explain themselves to one another or to anyone else. To make matters worse, they are in love with their various poses, with the theatrical possibilities of any occasion.

Coward lacks the elegant wit of Wilde, but he recognizes that for this type of play the main ingredients of style are clever insults, inverted commonplaces, and various *non-sequiturs*. He is also well aware of the values of visual effects as well as verbal ones. This is Judith's first entrance:

[*Enter Judith from the garden. She is carrying an armful of flowers and wearing a teagown, a large garden hat, gauntlet gloves, and goloshes.*]
Judith: You look awfully dirty, Simon. What have you been doing?
Simon [*nonchalantly*]: Not washing very much.
Judith: You should, darling, really. It's so bad for your skin to leave things about on it. [*She proceeds to take off her goloshes.*]

Sorel: Clara says Amy's got toothache.

Judith: Poor dear! There's some oil of cloves in my medicine cupboard. Who is Amy?

Sorel: The scullery maid, I think.

Judith: How extraordinary! She doesn't look Amy a bit, does she? Much more Flossie.—Give me a cigarette. [*Sorel gives her a cigarette and lights it.*] Delphiniums are those stubby red flowers, aren't they?

Simon: No, darling, they're tall and blue.

Judith: Yes, of course. The red ones are somebody's name—asters, that's it. I knew it was something opulent.

Coward's greatest successes in the play are the scenes in which Judith slips into the clichés of sentimental melodrama. The rest of the family cooperates; for, as Sorel says, "one always plays up to mother in this house; it's a sort of unwritten law." The most brilliant of all these scenes, one that combines almost all the comic motifs used, is that which follows Judith's discovery of David and Myra kissing. It is too long to quote in its entirety, but it ends like this:

Judith: David, I give you to her—freely and without rancor. We must all be good friends, always.

David: Judith, do you mean this?

Judith [*with a melting look*]: You know I do.

David: How can we ever repay you?

Judith: Just by being happy. I may leave this house later on—I have a feeling that its associations may become painful, especially in the autumn——

Myra: Look here, Judith——

Judith [*shouting her down*]: October is such a mournful month in England. I think I shall probably go abroad—perhaps a *pension* somewhere in Italy, with cypresses in the garden. I've always loved cypresses.

David: What about the children?

Judith: We must share them, dear.

David: I'll pay you exactly half the royalties I receive from everything, Judith.

Judith [*bowing her head*]: That's very generous of you.

David: You have behaved magnificently. This is a crisis in our lives, and thanks to you——

Myra [*almost shrieking*]: Judith—I *will* speak—I——

David: Ssshhh, Myra darling—we owe it to Judith to keep control of our emotions—a scene would be agonizing for her now. She has been brave and absolutely splendid throughout. Let's not make things harder for her than we can help. Come, we'll go out into the garden.

Myra: I will *not* go out into the garden.

Judith [*twisting her handkerchief*]: Please go—I don't think I can bear any more just now.

David: So this is the end, Judith?

Judith: Yes, my dear,—the end.

[*They shake hands sadly.*]

Like *The Importance of Being Earnest, Hay Fever* is satirical without being a satire. Coward enjoys ridiculing the clichés of sentimental romance as much as Wilde does, and both find stodgy conformity the worst of all evils. However, reform is not the object, but rather an escape, at least for the moment, into a realm of delightful irreverence and irresponsibility. Coward cannot always transmute insolence into ineffable poise, insult into epigram, or the inconsequent into crisis; but he can, while we remain in that enchanted hall at Cookham, hold us with the conviction that to be a poseur, to be cruelly rude and relentlessly egotistical is to be charming, witty, and altogether superior to the dullards who make up the rest of society. This effect is no mean achievement.

II Blithe Spirit

In *Blithe Spirit* (1941), Coward's finest example of a high farce and very possibly the best of all his plays, there is a balance between farcical plot and clever dialogue. The characters are no less waspish than those in *Hay Fever,* but they are not just playing a game. Nor is rudeness so obviously labeled grace.

Blithe Spirit concerns the consequences of an ill-considered séance. Charles Condomine, writer of mystery stories, has invited Madame Arcati, a professional medium, to conduct a séance so that he can observe her methods and collect some useful jargon for a story he is planning. Charles and his wife, Ruth, along with their guests, Dr. and Mrs. Bradman, expect to spend an amusing evening. All are convinced that Madame Arcati is either a charlatan or self-deluded. The séance, however, succeeds in materializing the spirit of Charles' first wife, Elvira; but she is visible and audible only to him. Ruth is at first convinced that Charles is playing some trick on her, then that he is mad, but is finally convinced of the shattering truth when Elvira condescends to move objects

about. Elvira decides to kill Charles so that he can join her in the
spirit world, but her plans go awry for it is Ruth who is killed
when the auto crashes. Madame Arcati attempts to dematerialize
Elvira, but succeeds only in bringing the spirit of Ruth onto the
scene. After many desperate efforts, Madame Arcati discovers that
Edith, the maid, is a Natural who has called the two spirits back
from the Other Side; now, with the medium's help, Edith succeeds in dematerializing them. Invisible but by no means exor-
cized, the two spirits commence to wreak havoc on the house as
Charles beats a retreat, convinced that the spirits cannot follow
him across the English Channel.

The comedy is primarily verbal. For example, when Elvira
makes her first appearance, Charles is startled enough to drop his
glass and to grow hysterical, but in a few moments he and the two
women are involved in a conversation that might be of the utmost
triviality except that Ruth, who cannot see or hear Elvira, has no
reason to believe that Charles isn't playing some kind of joke:

Ruth: Now sit down.

Charles: Why are you so anxious for me to sit down—what good
will that do?

Ruth: I want you to relax—you can't relax standing up.

Elvira: African natives can—they can stand on one leg for hours.

Charles: I don't happen to be an African native!

Ruth: You don't happen to be a *what?*

Charles [*savagely*]: An African native!

Ruth: What's that got to do with it?

Charles: It doesn't matter, Ruth—really it doesn't matter—we'll say
no more about it. [*He sits down.*] See, I've sat down.

Ruth: Would you like some more brandy?

Charles: Yes, please.

Elvira: Very unwise—you always had a weak head.

Charles: I could drink you under the table.

Ruth: There's no need to be aggressive, Charles—I'm doing my best
to help you.

Charles: I'm sorry.

Ruth [*bringing him some more brandy*]: Here—drink this—and
then we'll go up to bed.

Elvira: Get rid of her, Charles—then we can talk in peace.

Charles: That's a thoroughly immoral suggestion, you ought to be
ashamed of yourself.

Ruth: What is there immoral in that?

Ruth is momentarily shaken when Elvira's presence is conclusively demonstrated to her, but, apart from this, the rest of the
action is maintained on much the same level: Elvira pouting,
Ruth shrewish, Charles attempting to remain poised in the middle
of the two. Although a little stupid about grasping Elvira's motives, Charles is the articulate gentleman in any situation.

Brilliant as he can be in these skirmishes, Coward has exceeded
himself in the creation of Madame Arcati, a comic invention that
can well stand with Wilde's Lady Bracknell or Sheridan's Mrs.
Malaprop. A professional medium, she is also the author of whimsical children's stories "filled with highly conversational flora and
fauna" and of "enthusiastic biographies of minor royalties." In addition, she is a hearty bicyclist and is much given to what Ruth so
aptly calls "schoolgirl phraseology." From her first entrance, she
establishes herself as an utterly unpredictable mixture:

Madame Arcati: I'm afraid I'm rather late, but I had a sudden presentiment that I was going to have a puncture so I went back to fetch
my pump, and then of course I didn't have a puncture at all. . . .
Doctor Bradman—the man with the gentle hands! . . .
Charles: Would you like a cocktail?
Madame Arcati [*peeling off some rather strange-looking gloves*]: If
it's a dry Martini, yes—if it's a concoction, no. Experience has taught
me to be wary of concoctions.
Charles: It is a dry Martini.
Madame Arcati: How delicious. It was wonderful cycling through
the woods this evening—I was deafened by bird-song. . . .
Ruth: Don't you find it very tiring bicycling everywhere?
Madame Arcati: On the contrary—it stimulates me—I was getting
far too sedentary in London, that horrid little flat with the dim lights—
they had to be dim, you know, the clients expect it.
. . . . .
Ruth: Are you writing anything nowadays, Madame Arcati?
Madame Arcati: Every morning regular as clockwork, seven till one.
. . . It's a children's book—I have to finish it by the end of October
to catch the Christmas sales. It's mostly about very small animals, the
hero is a moss beetle. . . . I had to give up my memoir of Princess
Palliatini because she died in April—I talked to her about it the other
day and she implored me to go on with it, but I really hadn't the heart.

Madame Arcati's finest moments come in the last act, when she
sets about dematerializing the spirits. In the very last scene, after

five unsuccessful séances and any number of trances, she is ready to set to work once more.

Madame Arcati: Now then . . .
Charles: Now then what?
Madame Arcati: What do you say we have another seance and really put our shoulders to the wheel?—Make it a real rouser!
Elvira: For God's sake not another seance.
Madame Arcati: I might be able to materialize a trumpet if I tried hard enough—better than nothing, you know—I feel as fit as a fiddle after my rest.

John Gassner has called *Blithe Spirit* "a tour de force of fancy in which Coward also displays the cutting edge of his wit":

His, as Shaw might have said, is essentially "mindless" writing, but it would be difficult to match its cleverness. Many writers who pride themselves on the higher order of their cerebration might well envy Noel Coward's technical skill and showmanship. His showmanship is, indeed, so facile that it is arrogant. In *Blithe Spirit*, however, this is patently a virtue, not a defect. Coward carries off his trickery with a jaunty air, which is more than half the fun. If there are unappeasable souls who will persist in calling the play, along with other comedies by Coward, hollow, it is difficult to understand how they could fail to concede that it has very pleasant reverberations.[1]

III   I'll Leave It to You *and* The Young Idea

Noel Coward's other excursions into the realm of high farce have been few and of uneven success. Two of them are among his earliest works, *I'll Leave It to You* (1919), and *The Young Idea* (1921). The idea for the first was suggested by Gilbert Miller, the American producer, who had taken an interest in the young writer and was trying to get some of his work for production in the United States. *I'll Leave It to You* deals with a middle-aged bachelor who promises that he will leave his immense fortune to the one of his sister's lazy children who can most successfully carve out a career for himself. In very short order and when all are well on the way to deserving the inheritance and are discovering the pleasures of accomplishment in the process, it is revealed that Uncle Daniel is actually a pauper. At first infuriated, the young people soon see that the trick played on them was a wise one.

The Young Idea "was primarily inspired by Shaw's *You Never Can Tell*, Dolly and Philip being my original prototypes for Sholto and Gerda." The latter pair are brother and sister, in their late teens, "of the genus *enfant terrible*," who set about separating their father from his second wife and then bringing him back to their mother. They succeed after a series of complications doubly complicated by their taste for slipping into various theatrical roles, the idea which was to be given a far stronger and meaningful focus in *Hay Fever* (1924).

These two plays succeed in offering many opportunities for competent performers, and it comes as no surprise that Coward himself appeared in the first productions of both. Sholto (Coward's role) and Gerda are particularly attractive in their playacting. However, the plays fail in plot, at once commonplace in basic idea yet overly ingenious in construction, and in the style, which rarely makes the step from facetiousness to wit.

IV   Hands Across the Sea *and* Ways and Means

The years between *Hay Fever* (1924) and *Blithe Spirit* (1941) were extremely busy and prolific ones for Coward. Yet, except for two one-acts in *Tonight at 8:30*, he wrote no other examples of high farce during these years; but these two short plays, *Hands Across the Sea* and *Ways and Means*, are excellent high farces. *Hands Across the Sea* is set in the drawing-room of Lady Maureen Gilpin, called "Piggie" by her friends. She is terribly absent-minded and scatterbrained, yet dogmatic. On this afternoon, she has collected some of her elegant friends to meet the Rawlingsons, people she and her sister had stayed with in the Orient the year before. Instead, the Wadhursts, another colonial couple arrive; and it takes Piggie most of the play to discover her mistake and succeed, at the very last moment, in properly identifying her guests. Quietly, in the shadows, sits Mr. Burnham, a young man who has come to deliver some blueprints to Piggie's husband; and, as he leaves in the last seconds of the play, having decided merely to leave the plans on the table, Piggie is still under the assumption that he is the Wadhursts' son and bids him an affectionate goodbye.

The action is dominated by the telephone. Either Piggie or her sharp-tongued friend, Claire, is on the phone most of the time, gossiping about house-parties, quacking ducks performing at the

Café de Paris, pregnant friends, diets, and divorces. Between phone calls, or in the brief pauses in the telephone conversations, Piggie, Claire, and the other Londoners toss comments and questions at the Wadhursts, who grow progressively more bewildered. Finally, by telephone Piggie learns that the Rawlingsons cannot come after all; and the oblique, near-futile search for the Wadhursts' identity begins. Only as they leave, mentioning that they miss the theater in Pendarla, does Piggie triumphantly identify them and send them off using their names for the first time. When left alone, Piggie and Claire assure each other that the Wadhursts had a lovely time.

The laughter in *Hands Across the Sea* arises from the bewilderment of the provincials who are catapulted into a milieu in which trivia is enthroned and in which the art of unintentionally making the outsider miserable is perfected. In many ways, this pattern is that of *Hay Fever;* but here there is no intentional rudeness nor playacting, merely the abyss between cultures that belies the usual meaning of the title. And all is so fast and ludicrous that neither sympathy for the poor, bewildered colonials nor contempt for the gilded ephemera is possible.

In *Ways and Means,* the laughter depends on variations of deliberate insult. Stella and Toby Cartwright are an elegant young couple whose small income has barely kept them afloat as almost professional house-guests. Following a disastrous night at the Casino, they are without sufficient funds to move on to Venice, although they are being politely but inexorably evicted from the Villa Zephyre on the Côte d'Azur. Desperately, they pawn the few bits of jewelry they have left for a last chance at the Casino; but, just as Toby is about to play, Mrs. Irving Brandt, another guest at the Villa Zephyre, asks Toby if she may have his place, since the table is full. She quickly wins a fantastic amount of money, moves on, and Toby promptly loses everything he has. When all seems lost, the Cartwrights' room is entered by a burglar; they catch him, and he turns out to be Stevens, the just-cashiered chauffeur from a neighboring villa, desperate to steal the money from Mrs. Brandt. The Cartwrights will split it with him in return for protecting him. He carries out their instructions but insists on giving them all the money when he returns to their room, for he has also picked up some valuable jewels from Mrs. Brandt's table for his own use. He ties up the Cartwrights, and leaves them laughing behind their gags.

The play is in three scenes, but almost all the action is telescoped into the last few moments. The rest of the play is taken up with the Cartwrights' squabbling, first one and then the other insisting that each must "face facts" and "do something." The following is from the second scene, shortly after the Cartwrights' visit to the Casino, where they have lost everything including the money from pawning the bracelet left to Stella by her Aunt Agnes:

Stella: I was fond of Aunt Agnes and she was fond of me.
Toby: That rather cloying relationship belongs mercifully to the days before I met you.
Stella: She left me that bracelet in her will.
Toby: It seems odd that she should symbolize her almost incestuous love for you by such an undistinguished little trinket.

. . . . .

Stella: Aunt Agnes was the most generous woman in the world.
Toby: I suspect that your memory of her has been softened by time. To the impartial observer she appears to have been a mean old bitch.
Stella: Toby!
Toby: If it's all the same to you, I would prefer to leave Aunt Agnes where she rightly belongs, warbling through eternity with the Feathered Choir.
Stella: It seems a pity that you can't turn your devastating wit to a more commercial advantage—you should write a gossip column.
Toby: I haven't got a title.
Stella: Oh, shut up!
Toby: That was merely rude.

One must not, of course, be "merely rude"; cleverly rude, wittily rude, smartly rude—these are permissible ways to be and *Ways and Means* provides a well-stocked sample case.

V   Relative Values

Coward's next full-length high farce after *Blithe Spirit* was *Relative Values* (1951). *Blithe Spirit* is sub-titled *An Improbable Farce;* and, compared with that play, *Relative Values* appears solidly realistic. But, more than Coward's label, *A Light Comedy*, justifies inclusion of this play with the high farces. On the surface a comedy of manners with a satirical thrust at the decay of class distinctions, the play depends on a plot created by an extreme coincidence, on very broadly drawn characters whose motivations are generally of the thinnest, and on dialogue so well-bred and epigrammatic as to sound like a parody of the very highest of high comedies.

The setting of *Relative Values* is the living-room of Marshwood House. Felicity, Countess of Marshwood, is awaiting the arrival of her son, Nigel, and his bride-to-be, Miranda Frayle, a motion-picture star. Already concerned about her son's taste in women (his first wife was a frightful bore, and he has had a number of unpleasant mistresses), Felicity is startled to learn that Miranda is the young sister of Mrs. Moxton (Moxie), the Countess's invaluable maid. To shield Moxie from embarrassment, it is decided to pretend that, an uncle in Australia having left her a large fortune, Moxie has decided to remain at Marshwood House as a friend and companion. Miranda arrives and, not recognizing her sister, soon launches into an account of her childhood—a lugubrious tale punctuated with details of her sufferings at the hands of an alcoholic mother and sister, both now blessedly in their graves. This recital is more than Moxie can stand, and she reveals the truth. The convenient arrival of Don Lucas, Miranda's on- and off-screen lover, makes Felicity's task much easier; and Miranda is soon on her way to London.

The tone of the play is defined by the butler, Crestwell, one of the most prescient and articulate of all stage butlers. Informed of the relationship between Moxie and Miranda, a fact he had already deduced by himself, he says:

Crestwell: A coincidence in the best tradition of English high comedy, my Lady. Consider how delightfully Mr. Somerset Maugham would handle the situation!

Peter: I can think of other writers who wouldn't exactly sneeze at the idea.

Crestwell: If I may say so, sir, our later playwrights would miss the more subtle nuances. They are all too brittle. Comedies of manners swiftly become obsolete when there are no longer any manners.

Crestwell is quite right in saying that the situation is more like one of Maugham's comedies than like one of Coward's. The contrast between classes and generations has something of the quality of

Our Betters, although Coward reverses the coin, his sympathies lying with the Countess and with Crestwell, who are sensible, clear-eyed supporters of class hierarchies. Even more, the style and the cast of characters are reminiscent of Maugham; despite his reputation for elegant wit, Coward had never before dealt with the aristocrats of artificial comedy.

And like Maugham, and of course like the whole line of English high-comedy writers stretching back at least to the Restoration dramatist, George Etherege, Coward equates true aristocracy with aplomb, wit, and grace—the poise of the well-born and well-bred. As a result, *Relative Values* is distinguished from most Coward comedies in that it has far more quips and epigrams than usual. For example, Felicity says to one of her friends who has grown inarticulate with shock at the forthcoming marriage: "Dearest Cynthia. You really must not let righteous indignation play such hell with your syntax." Or there is Felicity on her first daughter-in-law: "She used to walk across a ballroom as if she were trudging through deep snow."

But the sharpest epigrams are assigned to Crestwell, the detached and cynical observer. Explaining to one of the servants why Moxie had dinner with the gentry, he says: "It is a social experiment based on the ancient and inaccurate assumption that, as we are all equal in the eyes of God, we should therefore be equally equal in the eyes of our fellow creatures. . . . The fact that it doesn't work out like that and never will in no way deters the idealists from pressing on valiantly toward Utopia. . . . A spiritually hygienic abstraction, Alice, where everyone is hail-fellow-well-met and there is no waiting at table." He ends the play with a toast, alone on the stage with Moxie: "The final inglorious disintegration of the most unlikely dream that ever troubled the foolish heart of man—Social Equality."

It is an appropriate toast for Crestwell, but one can well doubt if the play is really about social equality. Crestwell is indeed accurate in asserting that the later playwrights are too brittle and fail to capture the nuances. Just as *Easy Virtue* resembles a Pinero play without actually generating the serious concern that still gives *The Second Mrs. Tanqueray* some traces of vitality, *Relative Values* resembles a Maugham social comedy but without any serious concern about the issues involved.

Far more important than social issues are the farcical complications: Lady Hayling asking Moxie to sew on a button when Moxie is being passed off as an heiress; Miranda's habit of calling all her lovers, and asking them all to call her, Pete: Don Lucas standing in open-mouthed astonishment as Crestwell addresses him in rolling periods; Felicity's ingenuity in inventing tales to cover some of Moxie's slips; and, of course, the hilarious, explosive tension created by Moxie's listening to Miranda's fabrications about her childhood. What serious social implications the story may have are muted. None of which, however, lessens the success of *Relative Values* as an exercise in artificial comedy so highly polished that it almost seems to be reflecting the real world rather than wonderful shadows.

VI South Sea Bubble

Coward mounted another attack on social equality in *South Sea Bubble* (1955). Originally written in 1949 and titled *Home and Colonial,* this play was revised, retitled *Island Fling,* and presented for a few weeks in two American summer theaters in 1951. The final version, the only one available in print, was presented in London in 1956.

South Sea Bubble is set on the island of Samolo, a British possession in the Pacific, that is governed by Sir George Shotter, whose sympathies lie with the Samolan Socialist Nationals, who want self-government and the end of class distinctions. Punalo Alani and Hali Alani, father and son, are the leaders of the People's Imperial Party, who prefer benevolent imperialism and are particularly concerned that Sir George veto the bill that would make Public Conveniences free. This conflict is soon submerged in farcical complications that have little to do with the political theme.

Lady Alexandra Shotter, Sandra, is encouraged by her husband to try her womanly charm on Hali Alani to get him to change his position on the Public Conveniences bill. Cuckoo Honey, the bigoted, outspoken wife of the colonial secretary, is shocked by the sight of Sandra and Hali together; and she criticizes Sandra. Incensed, Sandra arranges for Hali to drive her to a party at a nearby night club; and afterwards she allows him to drive her to his beach cottage. There, with the help of the potent native brew and some savage drum playing, Hali attempts to seduce her; but she hits him with a bottle, steals his car keys, and gets home. The next day, Punalo Alani, having discovered Sandra's brooch, returns it with a plausible story; and all, on the best of terms, go in for lunch.

What is to be made of this action? That Coward is in sympathy with the wise Punalo is clear; even a blackmail attempt is presented as an only slightly disgraceful strategy in a good fight. Still, nothing much is resolved by the end of the play; and little is even examined. John Blair-Kennedy, a visiting novelist of the Maugham type, in reply to the comment that the modern idea is to treat even the most backward peoples' as equals, says, "The really modern idea is that we should treat them all as superiors." It is a witty line, and Blair-Kennedy has most of the witty lines; but its relevance to the play is even more questionable than Crestwell's oracular sayings are to *Relative Values.* Nor are the farcical elements very successful. The seduction scene and its consequences are unpredictable only insofar as they take place in an exotic locale; otherwise, the last half of the play might be by Sardou. If Coward means the episode to have some application to the question of self-government, public conveniences, or any other political or social question, his intention is lost.

Relative Values and *South Sea Bubble,* which form a revealing pair, demonstrate the very thin line between success and failure. *South Sea Bubble* has scenes which are very funny, but the play lacks any unifying plot, theme, or even character. Sandra is the leading character but even her actions lack consistency. Both plays state a point of view and neither develops it very much: In *Relative Values* it is the icing on the cake, decorative but dispensable; in *South Sea Bubble* the social problem is at first presented as if it were to be the main course but is then struck from the menu. The main failing, however, is in tone and manner. *Relative Values* is always eminently civilized, the living room of Marshwood House a familiar patch of ground where most characters are gifted with a marvelous fluency; where most problems can be discussed and solved in measured sentences; where manners, or the best mannerisms, are what really matter. Coward had no such pattern for *South Sea Bubble,* and the result is an unstable mixture of drawing-room badinage and unlikely echoes of Leon Gordon's *White Cargo* (1923).

VII   Nude with Violin

Coward's most recent venture into high farce is *Nude with Violin* (1954), a poor example. Based on the hoary idea that some greatly admired avant-garde art is a monstrous hoax, Coward's variations do little but underline the emptiness of the basic premise.

Following the funeral of Paul Sorodin, avant-garde painter *par excellence,* his family, his dealer, and his valet Sebastien gather in his studio. The family and Jacob Friedlander, the art dealer, discuss what is to be done about the valet. They decide to offer him a pension, but he has a surprise for them. Although there was no will, Sorodin did leave a witnessed letter in which he announces that he did not paint any of the pictures ascribed to him. The rest of the play concerns the various people who did paint them and their blackmailing the family by threatening exposure: there is a fake Russian princess, an English chorus girl, a Jamaican Negro, and, finally, when everything seems just about settled and hushed up, Sebastien's own schoolboy son. Having served the family so well in his suavely sinister way—for it is he who manages to satisfy all the "artists" and keep the family and Friedlander in the clear—Sebastien is now also chief benefactor.

The justification for Sorodin's forty-year masquerade was his "fanatical, burning hatred of dishonesty." To Sebastien, "He loathed cant, jargon, intellectual snobbery and the commercialising of creative talent. Successful art-dealers, critics and so-called experts were his bêtes noires. His detestation of them was almost pathological. . . . Creative talent was his god. He worshipped it ardently, passionately, all the more perhaps because he knew he hadn't a vestige of it himself. Far and away above everything else, he loved good painting. . . . He was a crusader."

When the Sorodins decide that perhaps it would be better to expose the truth than surrender to Sebastien's plan to pay the blackmailers, Sebastien draws the ironic moral:

Not only will *he* be disappointed, the whole world of modern painting will be humiliated and impoverished. The casualties in Hollywood alone will be appalling. The bottom will fall out of the market and thousands of up and coming young artists will starve. It will be a cataclysm! Many of the great masters too will be flung into disrepute, their finest pictures will be viewed with suspicion and distrust. If the news leaks out that the great Sorodin's masterpieces were painted by a Russian tart, an ex-Jackson Girl, an Eleventh Hour Immersionist and a boy of fourteen, the rot will spread like wildfire. Modern sculpture, music, drama and poetry will all shrivel in the holocaust. Tens of thousands of industrious people who today are earning a comfortable livelihood by writing without grammar, composing without harmony and painting without form, will be flung into abject poverty or forced really to learn their jobs. Reputations will wither overnight. No one will be spared. Not even Grandma Moses.

(Coward does a characteristic job of covering his seriousness with the next line when Isobel says, "I see no reason to drag in the Old Testament.")

These arguments are not only meretricious in themselves but seriously damage the fabric of the whole play. In the farce Coward has tried to construct, the speech about cant is embarrassingly sentimental and rings false. Such splendid motives might support a brief hoax followed by an exposé or some other means of crusading; but, after a lifetime of very profitable pretence, Sorodin's decision to leave the secret in the hands of the cynical Sebastien is evidence either of senility or of motives quite other than those attributed to him. The second of the speeches is a case of the author's face suddenly and shockingly appearing from behind the mask; and, while less objectionable in its logic, it is even more disturbing to the play's tone than is the first.

Most of this unconvincing preaching could be overlooked—comedies, especially farces, need not be exceptionally strong on logic or morality—if the play as a whole achieved a logic and morality of its own. The key to its failure is Sebastien, another of those "whacking good parts," but a thoroughly synthetic one. A compound of wildly incongruous pieces—admirable Crichton mixed with international thief, fluent in fourteen languages and accentless in all, apparently bi-sexual—he remains a compound rather than a creation; moreover, his *deux ex machina* machinations become tiresome and utterly predictable. The same effect is made by his wit, which in the beginning is as sharply pointed as anything Coward ever wrote. Sebastien, at the opening of the play, is, for example, being interviewed by Clinton Preminger, Junior, reporter from *Life:*

Clinton: You are of mixed parentage.

Sebastien: You have a genius for understatement, monsieur.

Clinton: Born in Martinique, date uncertain.

Sebastien: My whole life has been uncertain.

Clinton [*still at his notes*]: Deported from Syria in 1929. No offence specified.

Sebastien: The Syrians are terribly vague.

Clinton: Imprisoned in Saigon 1933. Offence specified.

Sebastien [*reminiscently*]: I remember it well.

Clinton: Resident in England 1936.

Sebastien: The happiest time of my life.

Clinton: Landed in Los Angeles 1937.

Sebastien: The saddest.

Clinton: Married in Rio de Janeiro 1939. Wife living.

Sebastien: With a customs officer.

Clinton: From 1942 to 1946, proprietor of a rooming-house in Mexico City.

Sebastien: Your delicacy does you credit, monsieur. . . .

However, this snide, snappy-comeback technique soon becomes wearing because Sebastien's opponents are without exception so utterly doltish that they are unable to recognize that Sebastien is their superior; and his persistent pin pricks can never do much but feed an egregious sense of hauteur. Although Isobel's talent for irrelevant reminiscence and the various approaches taken by the blackmailers afford some diversion, they quickly weaken before the onslaught of Sebastien's relentless cleverness. Coward's best comedies demonstrate the triumph of manner over trivial matter, magnificent sleights of hand; *Nude with Violin*, unfortunately, is mostly mannerism brewed with unpleasant subject matter that refuses to obey the magician and dissolve into thin air.

VIII   Fallen Angels

In the field of high comedy, as distinct from high farce, Coward has been busier and more consistently successful. In the comedy of manners, the characters inhabit the real world, albeit a very limited and special part of it. The setting, both physically and psychologically, is the drawing room, where life imitates art. The people who normally spend their time here are generally in their thirties, healthy, handsome, and wonderfully articulate. What the characters do exercise themselves about is usually sex: not passion, which is relegated to the bedroom if it is supposed to exist at all, but verbal skirmishing between those who would be, are or have been lovers, while a chorus of onlookers provides additional comment. The author's point is usually to castigate conventionality but gently and with the certainty that his audience is already on his side.

The artificiality of the comedy of manners must be a possible artificiality, the world of Mayfair or Park Avenue carefully weeded, pruned, and insect-proofed, but Mayfair and Park Avenue nonetheless. It must be highly selective realism, neither naturalism on the one hand nor pure fantasy on the other. It follows, therefore, that the situations and the characters must also be possible. The value given to them in the comedy of manners should be not too unlike what they would receive offstage. Jack Worthing and Algernon Montcrieff would be insufferable frauds in real life, but that handsome, beautifully dressed, and intelligent-looking woman sitting across the aisle at the opera might be Maugham's Constance Middleton (*The Constant Wife*). Motivation may be thin, but it must be credible.

As with every other type of writing he has done, Coward's first attempts at the comedy of manners date from the very earliest days of his writing career. The first example of which there is any record is a one-act entitled *The Better Half* (1921). The heroine, Alice, feels herself cursed with a husband of such broad-minded complacency that she will do anything to knock him off his self-made pedestal. She finally arouses him by accusing him of using his pose of imperturbability and high idealism to attract the admiration and devotion of susceptible women. When the friend who is in love with the husband enters, Alice gives each to the other and storms out, announcing that she will take a lover and make it easy for the husband to secure a divorce. The husband delivers the curtain line: "To my mind, we should all try to make ourselves see things from every point of view."

Coward comments that "it was quite well written and served the purpose, if only for a little, of keeping my name before the public." [2] Even in outline, the play also indicates some characteristic Coward patterns: the self-assured egotist who can be the object of attack when his egotism is not lightened by ironic awareness; the squabble and/or harangue as the central episode of the play; and the probing for weaknesses in a conventionally ideal marriage—indeed, the suggestion that the course of true love cannot, *should* not run smooth.

Coward's first distinguished drawing room comedy, *Fallen Angels* (1923), a full-length one that in fact takes place in a dining room, was also written before that momentous day that *The Vortex* opened; but it was not produced until the following year. The plot structure is very slight. Julia Sterrol and Jane Banbury have both received postcards announcing the imminent arrival of Maurice Duclos, a debonair Frenchman to whom each had been mistress (first Julia, then Jane) before their marriages. Luckily, the two husbands have left London for a weekend of golf, and the ladies decide to run away. They are stopped by a ring of the doorbell; it turns out to be the plumber, but Julia and Jane are startled into seeing the foolishness of their attempt to escape. Instead, they plan a welcoming dinner for Maurice. They want the situation to seem as if he has stumbled into a scene of domestic happiness and calm and as if his announcement has not panicked them in the least.

When Maurice does not appear, they begin to eat; more to the point, they begin to drink the cocktails, champagne, and liqueurs that had been ordered for their guest. As the women grow more intoxicated, they become suspicious of each other's present intentions, until Jane announces that she knows where Maurice is and rushes out to join him. The next morning, the husbands return, having quarreled on the golf course; and, when Jane appears in bedraggled evening dress, the truth begins to come out. At this point, Maurice arrives, grasps the situation at once, and laughingly tells them that the whole thing was engineered by the wives to restimulate the husbands' ardor. Convinced, Fred and Willy allow their wives to go to Maurice's new apartment, which is on the floor above, to help him select curtains; but the play ends as they hear, with some discomfort, the strains of their wives' favorite song, together with its first line: "Même les Anges succombent à l'amour."

The best scene in the play is the one in which the two women become drunk, for they move imperceptibly from tense apprehension to meditative reminiscence, thence to hysterical giggling, and finally to bitter quarreling. This scene calls for virtuoso actresses for whom Coward has provided a sturdy underpinning of dialogue. Much depends on wrong-number telephone calls, on taxi sounds outside, and on other mechanical interruptions and delays —all of them handled so smoothly and easily that there is little sense of contrivance. The first act of *Fallen Angels* is too long for the small amount of exposition needed, and the third act is somewhat psychologically implausible; but the second act is among Coward's most successful duologues.

Fallen Angels aroused a good deal of vituperation which Coward found startling; and although he stoutly denies the charge of immorality, he does conclude that the play is not "one of my best comedies but it is gay and light-hearted." The complaints, including "a mass of insulting letters from all parts of the country," [3] were stimulated by Coward's introducing characters and situations most indecorous if measured by the standards of the Maugham theater. Today, four decades after the play was written, Coward's leading ladies seem rather pale beside the wantons of William Wycherley or the heroines of Tennessee Williams; but the play nonetheless stands up quite well. Coward may very well have underrated it.

IX This Was a Man, The Marquise, *and* Home Chat

In the two years following the production of *Fallen Angels,* Coward wrote three more comedies: *This Was a Man* (1926); *The Marquise* (1926); and *Home Chat* (1927); and none was very successful. *This Was a Man* concerns Edward Churt, a popular portrait painter. His wife, Carol, has been systematically unfaithful to him; he knows it but feels unsure about what to do. The post-war world he lives in has complacently accepted adultery, but divorce is still an unpleasant and public business. His friend, Major Evelyn Bathurst, assuming that Edward is unaware of Carol's infidelity, decides to teach her a lesson. When he invites her to his flat with the intention of scolding and humiliating her, she uses the opportunity for thoroughly confusing and ultimately seducing him. Unflinchingly righteous to the end, Bathurst tells Edward the truth; but Edward, who has just finished lecturing Carol himself, bursts into laughter. Finally, he orders Carol to leave the country, in which case he will give her grounds for divorce; otherwise, he will divorce her, naming Bathurst as corespondent. He then blithely leaves for lunch with Zoe St. Merryn, the sensible, worldly woman he should have married in the first place.

For a picture of post-war morality, the basic structure of the play is promising; and there are moments when the dialogue throws some illumination on the moral questions raised by the plot. However, most of the play is virtually a parody of Coward's mannerisms: An immense amount of time is devoted to offering cigarettes, accepting cigarettes, lighting cigarettes, and smoking cigarettes. Between cigarettes, there is time for offering and accepting drinks, announcing the arrival of new guests, and bidding adieus. And whether cigarettes or adultery is under discussion, the characters rely almost entirely on a tight-lipped stichomathia in which the average sentence is about five words long. For example:

Evelyn: Are you ever sentimental about anything?
Carol: Do I seem so hard?
Evelyn: A little, I think.
Carol: I'm not, really.
Evelyn: I'm afraid Edward's unhappy.
Carol: Not deep down inside.
Evelyn: Are you sure?
Carol: He may think he is.
Evelyn: Poor Edward.

The Marquise is better, but the play never quite rises above being a clever, competent exercise in eighteenth-century comedy that is written from a distinctly twentieth-century point of view. The Marquise Eloise de Kestournel, on a September evening in the year 1735, makes a surprise appearance at the Château de Vriaac and suggests to Raoul, Comte de Vriaac, her former lover, that he take her as his wife. The Comte is more than startled since he has assumed that Eloise was dead, since he has reared their daughter Adrienne to believe that she was the child of his late wife, and since he has just announced the betrothal of Adrienne to the son of his closest friend, Esteban, El Duco de Santaguano. Eloise has already learned that Adrienne and her betrothed are not in love with each other and that the girl is in love with the Comte's secretary. The next day, when she recognizes Esteban as another of her lovers, she learns that *their* child is Miguel, the fiancé. When neither the Comte nor Esteban is present, she forces Father Clement to marry Adrienne and the secretary and sends them off to Paris.

Later, when Esteban returns, he finds Raoul drunk. Soon they are comparing notes, discovering the ways in which they were both involved with Eloise. When they quarrel and begin to duel, Eloise stops the duel, reconciles the men, and announces that she is waiting for one of them to fulfill their identical promises. Esteban gallantly proposes, but he is relieved when the Comte's declaration of love reveals that his feelings go far deeper than mere gallantry. Eloise is left, therefore, with her true love.

It is surprising that *The Marquise* has not had a more successful stage career, especially among non-professionals. There is only one setting, which can but need not be elaborate; the investment in costumes is minimal; the three leading roles lend themselves very well to a display of stylized "period" posturing that is so much easier for actors to manage than the nuances of true eighteenth-century style; and the whole play manages to maintain a pleasant balance between a smart, amoral sophistication and the conventional pieties (true love wins out at last, and Eloise is in some vague way more saint than sinner). Perhaps if Coward had not so soon after the production of *The Marquise* presented, in rapid succession, one of his best revues, *This Year of Grace!;* the best of his sentimental operettes, *Bitter-Sweet;* and one of the most brilliant of his comedies, *Private Lives,* the appeals of his costume piece would not have been so quickly forgotten.

Before *This Year of Grace!* (1928), *Home Chat* (1926) appeared. The basic idea is that circumstantial evidence can be more convincing than the truth, and Coward contrived to demonstrate it by having most of his characters assume guilt when the parties involved are innocent, and vice versa. Characters Janet Ebony and Peter Chelsworth have shared a *wagon-lit* compartment because of a confusion of tickets on a very crowded train. When a dreadful accident occurs, Janet and Peter, the only survivors in their carriage, are rescued in their pajamas. After Janet and Peter arrive at her house, they find waiting for them her husband, Paul, a popular novelist, his mother, Janet's mother, and Lavinia Hardy, Peter's fiancée—and all assume that Janet and Peter have been having an affair, and no amount of explaining will convince them of the truth. When Paul in his loftiest Olympian manner assures Janet that he forgives her and is ready to talk things over "coolly and sensibly," Janet storms out of the house. She and Peter act the roles of illicit lovers until Alec Stone, a friend of Peter's, makes them see how foolish such action is.

In the last act, the family once more awaits Janet's return from Paris, convinced that she has been there with Peter. They are startled when Peter arrives with Lavinia, whom he has just married. He explains the stunt that Janet had been playing on them; so, when Janet returns and tries to tell them that she has been having an affair in Paris with Alec Stone, everyone believes she is still joking. However, in her absence, Paul has discovered that he loves Mavis Wittersham, with whom he has long had a Platonic friendship. He takes the initiative in suggesting a divorce. Janet agrees, amusedly playing the magnanimous injured party.

"It was obvious last night that the gallery did not take to the cynical ending—the husband pairing off with a woman who had aspired to be his soul-mate, and the wife beginning, as the final curtain descended, a tender conversation over the telephone with the Guards officer with whom she had spent a week in Paris." [4] This cynical end, meant to be poetic justice, is a less serious weakness than the meagerness and illogic of the whole play. Most of the second act, usually the jewel in a Noel Coward play for which the first and third acts provide the setting, is taken up with Janet's and Peter's playing lovers—an implausible situation. Janet Ebony is far too perceptive a woman to go on with such a childish game, even if it seemed sensible in the first moments of rage. Moreover, except for the introduction of Alec, the scene is virtually a repeat of the first act; for the two mothers and Lavinia once more reach the wrong conclusion. This time, however, the scorn heaped upon them is hardly justified since Janet and Peter have tried to give the impression that they are having an affair. Finally, the sub-plot involving Paul and Mavis is too obvious and silly; borrowing elements from the story of D. H. Lawrence—Mavis calls her soul-mate "Paulo"—and applying every cliché borrowed from the stereotype of the yearning, pseudo-intellectual spinster, Coward has only created a caricature so transparent that even Paul would hardly be deceived.

X Private Lives

Considering that Coward had been performing on stage since 1911 and that he had frankly admitted his interest in writing effective roles for himself, it is surprising that he did not appear in one of his own comedies of manners until 1930. This may explain many of the weaknesses of *Home Chat, The Marquise,* and *This Was a Man,* since the plays without Coward roles are frequently his weakest. If, in addition, there are roles for some of the actresses and actors with whom he most delights in working, extraordinary results can safely be forecast. Nowhere is this more true than in *Private Lives* (1929), written for Coward and Gertrude Lawrence, and *Design for Living* (1932), with Coward, Lynn Fontanne, and Alfred Lunt.

Coward's rapport with Gertrude Lawrence must have been extraordinary indeed (as *Tonight at 8:30* also bears out), for what had been sources of weakness in some of the earlier plays now become, in *Private Lives,* the groundwork for one of the best. The plot is slight. Elyot Chase and Amanda Prynne, five years after their divorce, meet again in Deauville on the night when each is beginning a honeymoon with a second spouse. In adjoining rooms at the hotel, they meet on the balcony outside. Immediately attracted to each other again, they abandon Deauville and run off to Amanda's flat in Paris. There they re-establish the pattern that had destroyed their marriage, moments of rapture alternating with increasingly ugly quarrels. Elyot's second wife, Sybil, and Amanda's second husband, Victor, arrive at the flat to find not only the place in shambles but Elyot and Amanda pummeling each other on the floor. At first, it seems that Elyot and Amanda will once more separate; but, as Sybil and Victor begin to wrangle, Elyot and Amanda go away together once more.

The talk is brilliant, for Elyot and Amanda are equals; they form one of the few modern equivalents of the witty couple so favored by the Restoration dramatists. In style, they differ a good deal from, say, Congreve's pairs—they are a good deal more facetious and bad-tempered—but there is the same exhilarating presence of two elegant figures whose minds produce sparks when rubbed together. For them, Coward has even succeeded in creating a love scene which is at once witty and sincere, not, as is too often the case, irritatingly arch and cloying.

The supreme achievement of the play is the second act when, except for a very few moments, Elyot and Amanda are alone on stage. As Coward did in *Fallen Angels,* he has allowed the scene to develop slowly to its shattering finale. He even repeats the device of a wrong-number telephone call. This scene is, however, even more challenging; for there is no problem to cause tension or suspense. True, Elyot and Amanda expect their respective partners to discover them in time, but they are not particularly concerned. Instead, the pressure comes from within as each surrenders to the promptings of the imp of malice and the desire to have the last word. Here is a sample from early in the scene, the beginning of the first quarrel:

Amanda: When we were together, did you really think I was unfaithful to you?

Elyot: Yes, practically every day.

Amanda: I thought you were too; often I used to torture myself with visions of you bouncing about on divans with awful widows.

Elyot: Why widows?

Amanda: I was thinking of Claire Lavenham really.

Elyot: Oh Claire.

Amanda [*sharply*]: What did you say "Oh Claire" like that for? It sounded far too careless to me.

Elyot [*wistfully*]: What a lovely creature she was.

Amanda: Lovely, lovely, lovely!

Elyot [*blowing her a kiss*]: Darling!

Amanda: Did you ever have an affair with her? Afterward I mean?

Elyot: Why do you want to know?

Amanda: Curiosity, I suppose.

Elyot: Dangerous.

Amanda: Oh not now, not dangerous now. I wouldn't expect you to have been celibate during those five years, any more than I was.

Elyot [*jumping*]: What?

Their anger quickly mounts; and, although they soon manage to stop the quarrel, the pattern has been set: the act develops through a sequence of ever more violent and irreconcilable altercations, until both are on the floor "rolling over and over in paroxysms of rage."

The play is a bravura piece for two. Sybil and Victor are only sufficiently real to provide momentary relief and ammunition for Elyot and Amanda. Thus Ivor Brown's comments on the first night seem accurate:

Within a few years the student of drama will be sitting in complete bewilderment before the text of *Private Lives,* wondering what on

earth those fellows in 1930 saw in so flimsy a trifle. Well, they saw
Mr. Coward as actor and producer and they saw Miss Gertrude Lawrence; in short they saw a species of magic. The first attribute of a
successful magician is cheek; nerves, shame, hesitation are unknown
to him. He must trust implicitly in his wrist and his rabbit. Mr. Coward
has exactly the right effrontery for a first-rate conjuror, and a first-rate
conjuror, be it added, is a first-rate artist of the theatre. . . . The
seeming spontaneity of the chatter has only been attained by the most
industrious stage-craft and a remarkable sense of timing and of tones.
The success lies in giving the charade illusion. There is little enough
in Mr. Coward's text; there is everything up his sleeve. . . . The result is all shimmer and spangles with a little slapstick—in short, Harlequinade *à la mode*.[5]

But the play has something more than transient magic, a good
deal more; for bewilderment has not set in. The Harlequinade
spirit dominates the printed page as much as it does the performance. Mr. Brown is only one of the innumerable reviewers and
critics who have underestimated the power of Coward's plays in
print, apparently because the performances were always so impressive. Surely any reader with even a minimal ability to imagine
the play in production can respond to the shimmer and spangles.
It is not the theme which holds our interest, nor character, nor
plot, nor even wit in its usual sense of clever statements quotable
out of context. There is enough of all of these to provide coherence and easy laughter, but it is his ability to capture on paper the
sense of innocent playfulness, the "charade illusion," and a delight
in that playfulness that belies Coward's own comment that *Private Lives* is only "a reasonably well-constructed dualogue for two
experienced performers." If "innocent playfulness" seems a
strange phrase to apply to a play dealing with bad-tempered,
world-weary adulterers, it is this very paradox that gives the play
its vitality.

XI Design for Living

The Lunts, although expert farceurs, had established themselves as actors who dealt only in plays of some substance,
whether serious or comic: in the 1920's they had worked almost
exclusively with the Theatre Guild in such plays as Ferenc
Molnar's *The Guardsman*, Franz Werfel's *Goat Song*, Eugene
O'Neill's *Strange Interlude* (Miss Fontanne creating the central

role of Nina Leeds), and Robert Sherwood's *Reunion In Vienna.*
Design for Living (1932), the play Coward wrote for himself and
the Lunts is, not surprisingly, a good deal more serious in intent
than is *Private Lives;* more than any other comedy of Coward's, it
deliberately raises and discusses questions about morality in more
than a passing, light-hearted way.

The central figure in *Design for Living* is Gilda, a beautiful,
intelligent young woman who intermittently works as an interior
decorator. A few years before the play opens, she had met Otto, a
painter, and Leo, a playwright. The two men have been very close
friends for a long time while living in the Latin Quarter. Gilda
loves them both; but, first drawn sexually to Otto, she has become
his mistress. When the play begins, it is the morning after Gilda
has succumbed to Leo, just back from America, where his play
has received a successful production. Otto has been away from
Paris for a few days; when he returns, he discovers what has happened and storms out, determined never to see either again.

Eighteen months later, Leo is enjoying tremendous celebrity in
London; and Gilda has become bitter about what she feels is his
surrender to adulation. When Otto reappears from a long ocean
voyage (he, too, is now a fashionable success), the pendulum
swings back once more. Gilda, panicked by this new situation and
disturbed by the change affluence has made in both men, runs
away. Another two years elapse. Gilda is now married to Ernest
Friedman, an art dealer. They live in a palatial penthouse in New
York, and now Gilda, too, is rich and successful. When Leo and
Otto come to call, Gilda panics once more and runs away; but she
returns the next day, ready to leave with the two friends for some
vague *ménage à trois.*

Aware that many people found the play unpleasant, although
they were entertained, Coward tried to explain the objections
away:

This sense of "unpleasantness" might have been mitigated for them
a little if they had realized that the title was ironic rather than dogmatic. I never intended for a moment that the design for living suggested in the play should apply to anyone outside its three principal
characters, Gilda, Otto, and Leo. These glib, over-articulate, and
amoral creatures force their lives into fantastic shapes and problems
because they cannot help themselves. Impelled chiefly by the impact
of their personalities each upon the other, they are like moths in a pool

of light, unable to tolerate the lonely outer darkness, and equally unable to share the light without colliding constantly and bruising one another's wings.[6]

But it can be said of any work of fiction that its working out can be applied in full only to the characters therein. So Coward has hardly answered the charge, since the choice of characters and their situation must strike many as unpleasant. Nor has Coward completely come to terms with the special situation he sets up.

Actually, there are two subjects. On the one hand, there is the dilemma created by the desires of two men, inseparable friends, who are in love with the same woman, who is equally attracted to both. At the same time, she feels a strong but ambiguous bond between herself and Ernest, the older, paternal figure. (John Howard Lawson points out the parallels with O'Neill's *Strange Interlude*: "Like Nina, [Gilda] requires three men; like Nina, she marries the conventional man whom she considers a fool." [7]) On the other hand, there is the theme of success. Act I is mostly taken up with the first subject, for Gilda's discovery of the full extent of her dual love occupies the center of the stage. Act II concentrates more on the second theme, as Gilda becomes disillusioned about both men.

Act III tries to fuse the two. Gilda is now also a success, hence independent, hence . . . but nothing follows. Gilda's life with Ernest has confirmed her feelings about the emptiness and sterility of wealth and position, but have the men achieved this realization? And if they have, what then? In the end it comes down to what Amanda Prynne called "chemical what d'you call 'ems." Even if the design is to apply to just these three, it remains a frustratingly vague design. What had started out as a premise— that such a three-cornered relationship is possible—is now accepted by the three principals as a truth. However, this truth is neither demonstrated, nor adequately discussed, and large sections of the play are about something equally unresolved: the theme of success.

The style and tone of the play also reflect its split personality. Act I is, despite some flashes of humor, largely serious. Act II shows a change. The first scene, with its telephone calls (usually answered by Leo in one of a variety of false, ridiculous accents), its cloddish newspaper reporter and Leo's dim-witted servant,

Miss Hodge, is light and satiric, hopping briskly from laugh to laugh. Scene two, between Gilda and Otto, is an extended love scene, witty and understated, in the manner of the first act of *Private Lives*. The third scene is a duet for Otto and Leo as they drink themselves into maudlin tears over Gilda's departure. The first scene of Act III takes a different tack. Leo and Otto arrive, "attired in very faultless evening dress"; and, discovering that Gilda has guests, they play at being hyper-sophisticated, ultra-insolent dandies because, they say, the others wouldn't go, "they were going to stay for ever and ever and ever!" The final scene is, once more, fairly serious.

Despite these weaknesses, *Design for Living* is one of Coward's most attractive and intriguing plays. For one thing, it has considerably more substance than other, smoother comedies. The triangle he has created may not be very intelligibly resolved, but he does take it seriously, not as a peg for ribald laughter; in fact the play is as free of double-entendres or sex jokes as it is of the other trappings of the bedroom farce. And, since Coward takes the situation seriously, he has outdone himself in the creation of at least one of the characters, Gilda.

Although Leo and Otto are well-nigh interchangeable with any of Coward's bright, flippant yet inherently sentimental men, Gilda is more than another Amanda Prynne, and other than a lighter version of Nina Leeds. She is truly intelligent, not just worldly; her anguish, particularly in Act I, is not just acute embarrassment and loss of poise; and her self-understanding goes a good deal deeper than Amanda's superficial contrition. Gilda, in fact, gives the play coherence and significance which any summary can only partly suggest. At the same time, this very solidity makes the ending so unsatisfactory; for Gilda should provide some insight into the situation. However, the best she can manage is an abstract evasion:

Why shouldn't I be a mad woman? I've been sane and still for two years. You were deceived by my dead behavior because you wanted to be. It's silly to go on saying to yourself that I'm different from Otto and Leo just because you want to believe it. I'm not different from them. We're all of a piece, the three of us. Those early years made us so. From now on we shall have to live and die our own way. No one else's way is any good, we don't fit.

It is difficult to argue with Lawson that the reason the play ultimately achieves little insight is that the author "believes that human behavior is irrational":

The feeling of the moment is beautiful because it is momentary. Thus the people inevitably come back, again and again, to the feeling already experienced, to renew the momentary sensation—and the only *design for living* is a design of neurotic repetition. These people are completely sentimental (because they depend entirely on feeling), and completely cynical (because their feelings are continually proved contradictory and valueless). Being deprived of conscious will, they are victims of fate, which dictates the twists and turns of feeling which constitute their lives.[8]

The play ends with Gilda, Otto, and Leo groaning and weeping with laughter at Ernest's outrage; but their laughter says very little except that the audience should also laugh.

The theme of success is often an excuse for light satire on newspaper gossip, celebrity hunting, and the like. Yet Coward goes beyond that when he considers the changes that success can bring. There is nothing novel, to say the least, about the conclusion that money and celebrity bring no happiness; but Coward refuses to present a black and white picture. Love among the artists is pleasant but only because the artist is willing, even eager, to sacrifice the present for a future success. Once success comes, there is no going back:

Otto: In the beginning, when we were all in Paris, everything was really very much easier to manage, even our emotional problems. Leo and I were both struggling, a single line was in both our minds leading to success—that's what we were planning for, working like dogs for! You helped us both, jostling us onto the line again when we slipped off, and warming us when we were cold in discouragement. You picked on me to love a little bit more, because you decided, rightly then, that I was the weaker. They were very happy, those days, and glamour will always cling to them in our memories. But don't be misled by them; don't make the mistake of trying to recapture the spirit of them. That's dead, along with our early loves and dreams and quarrels, and all the rest of the foolishness.

This rejection of nostalgia leaves the nagging question, "What now?" Having come as far as the following outburst near the end of Act II, Coward jettisons this theme:

Leo: Let's make the most of the whole business, shall we? [Gilda has just left them both.] Let's be photographed and interviewed and pointed at in restaurants! Let's play the game for what it's worth, secretaries and fur coats and de-luxe suites on transatlantic liners at minimum rates! Don't let's allow one shabby perquisite to slip through our fingers! It's what we dreamed many years ago and now it's within our reach. Let's cash in, Otto, and see how much we lose by it. . . . Success in twenty lessons! Each one more bitter than the last! More and better Success! Louder and funnier Success!

Coward returns to this idea with a somewhat clearer if less serious concern in *Present Laughter,* yet the strength with which these ideas make their appearance in *Design for Living* once more reveals that in this play, for once, he goes beyond the limits of brittle artifice.

XII   Present Laughter

"Life," says Otto in *Design for Living,* "is for living first and foremost. Even for artists, life is for living." This statement could stand as an epigraph to *Present Laughter* (1938), beside the quotation from Shakespeare's *Twelfth Night* which gives the play its title:

> What is love? 'tis not hereafter;
> Present mirth hath present laughter;
>   What's to come is still unsure:
> In delay there lies not plenty;
> Then come and kiss me, sweet and twenty,
>   Youth's a stuff will not endure.

Together, these statements summarize the theme of *Present Laughter.* Like *Design for Living, Present Laughter* "springs from a social philosophy . . . which regards pragmatic sensation as the only test of conduct," [9] but the play is presented with so bright and light an air that no nagging questions disturb one's pleasure.

Perhaps an annotated *dramatis personae* can serve to indicate at least some of the complexities of plot and subplot: Garry Essendine, a successful romantic actor, is a matinee idol. Slightly over forty and fully as egocentric as dashing actors are reputed to be, he is becoming very conscious of age, a consciousness which gives added impetus to his philandering. Liz Essendine, Garry's wife, but living apart from him, was once an actress; she is now a member of Garry's entourage, primarily engaged in writing or adapting plays for him, secondarily engaged in trying to keep his romantic life from getting out of hand. Joanna Lyppiat, Hugo's wife, is a predatory type, who becomes, first, Morris's mistress, then, for one night, Garry's. The effort to keep her presence in Garry's apartment unknown, and then Garry's decision to reveal the whole tangled relationship constitutes most of the action in the last half of the play. Daphne Stillington, one of the many young ladies to fall under the Essendine spell, differs from the others in remaining persistent even after Garry has used his well-rehearsed, normally unfailing, heart-tugging morning-after fare-well scene. Roland Maule is a young playwright from the provinces. When Garry is driven to tell Maule what he really thinks of the young man's pseudo-poetic, pseudo-profound play, the young man, instead of being insulted, finds himself virtually hypnotized by the older man and continues to push his way into Garry's studio at the most inopportune moments in order to be near this man whose "vibrations" are somehow of the utmost importance to his sanity. Monica Reed is Garry's cool, witty secretary; Miss Erikson, his maid, a Swedish spiritualist; Fred, his cheeky valet; Morris Dixon, his director, and Hugo Lyppiat, his producer.

Garry is preparing to go on a tour of Africa and at least half of the others arrive at the last moment to announce that they intend to accompany him. Complications, romantic and otherwise, are brushed aside at the end (but hardly resolved) by Garry, Liz, Morris, and Hugo, forgetting all other concerns as they quarrel about the choice of a theater for Garry's next London season.

The play is obviously not very profound. Yet the variety of characters and situations allows for a few moments in which Coward can drop easily and effectively into a mood of serious comment. The most revealing of these occasions is in the first act, where Coward, disguised as Essendine, is confronted by his severest critics, disguised as Roland Maule:

Roland: Every play you appear in is exactly the same, superficial, frivolous, and without the slightest intellectual significance. You have a great following and a strong personality, and all you do is prostitute yourself every night of your life. All you do with your talent is to wear

dressing-gowns and make witty remarks when you might be really
helping people, making them think! Making them feel! . . . If you
want to live in people's memories, to go down to posterity as an important man, you'd better do something about it quickly. There isn't
a moment to be lost.

Garry: I don't give a hoot about posterity. Why should I worry
about what people think of me when I'm dead as a doornail anyway?
My worst defect is that I am apt to worry too much about what people
think of me when I'm alive. But I'm not going to do that any more.
I'm changing my methods and you're my first experiment. As a rule,
when insufferable young beginners have the impertinence to criticize
me, I dismiss the whole thing lightly because I'm embarrassed for them
and consider it not quite fair game to puncture their inflated egos too
sharply. But this time, my highbrow young friend, you're going to get
it in the neck. To begin with, your play is not a play at all. It's a meaningless jumble of adolescent, pseudo-intellectual poppycock. It bears
no relation to the theatre or to life or to anything. . . . If you wish to
be a playwright you just leave the theatre of tomorrow to take care of
itself. Go and get yourself a job as a butler in a repertory company if
they'll have you. Learn from the ground up how plays are constructed
and what is actable and what isn't. Then sit down and write at least
twenty plays one after the other, and if you can get the twenty-first
produced for a Sunday-night performance you'll be damned lucky!

The play skips along from complication to complication, Garry
always at the center: beating his forehead at the betrayals by his
friends, suavely bidding farewell to young love, skirmishing with
Joanna, shouting at Maule, or bemusedly discussing Fred's private
life. As with all comedy roles created for Coward himself, Essendine has the gift of the most enviable fluency, whether he is being
waspish, sentimental, insulting, or merely clownish. He is, in fact,
the very embodiment of the figure we might call "Noel" (as Oscar
Wilde was Oscar, Max Beerbohm simply Max), that public image
of sophisticated insolence, self-confessed egotism, and of half-
concealed sentimentality.

    Present Laughter may also be the best example of Coward's
ability to keep a play bubbling even when there is no plot or
character development to give it movement. Motivation is mainly
a mirage. The key to most of the action is the tightly-knit fellowship of the Essendine production group who have "all been devoted to one another for many years"; but, unless we accept the
Cowardian premise that bitter quarreling is one of the surest signs

of love, the fellowship seems to be a thoroughly mercenary one. Joanna, the *femme fatale,* is hardly conceivable at all in logical terms. She is a "head-hunter" who will "make trouble," but beyond that there is not much point in asking questions. Maule, Daphne, Fred, and Monica are drawn from the stockpile.

Yet nothing matters much as the characters charge and countercharge, as complications are piled up. And by carefully maneuvering everybody off and on stage in a convincing fashion, by filling any possible blank spot or transition with a clever contrivance, and by making all but the most oafish characters glitter with wit, Coward keeps the pace rapid and the effect sparkling. This play superbly illustrates what J. C. Trewin has called "quick, *scratch-flare, scratch-flare* stuff, like a succession of lighted matches." [10]

XIII   Quadrille

Set in 1873, *Quadrille* (1951), begins and ends in the Buffet de la Gare, Boulogne:

The Marquess of Heronden and the wife of an American railway magnate pause at the station during their elopement to his French villa and later, in a sitting-room at Heronden House in Belgrave Square, the deserted wife and husband plan a pursuit. Surprising the lovers at the villa, their astute diplomacy shatters romantic illusions, and the respective marriages are perfunctorily resumed for another year. Then the inevitable happens and the Marchioness and the American pass through Boulogne on the way to start a new life together.[11]

Coward is concerned with little more than this reassortment, and in line with his title he has made the play as symmetrical as possible. Each eloping couple takes the same table at the buffet and meets the same English clergyman and his ludicrous family. Serena, the marchioness, is gossiping with her friend, Lady Harriet Ripley, when she opens the note announcing her husband's departure; and she is gossiping with Harriet as she prepares her own note for her husband. Coward has always liked neatly symmetrical effects, but nowhere else has he made them so obvious, so much part of the elegant artificiality of the whole.

Setting and story go beautifully together. This is not Victorian England, of course, but a selected view, part Oscar Wilde, part Constantin Guys, part Henry James. Hubert, the Marquess of Heronden, is incurably romantic; but he is so in the sense that the

exquisite dandy is a romantic, and not in Shelley's way. Serena is
full of charm and wit, which "mask an executive determination
that would shame Napoleon Bonaparte." Axel Diensen, an unpol-
ished American, is crude and explosive in manner but capable of a
forceful eloquence:

> My vocabulary is boundless. I can curse the stars out of the sky
> with rich words that you do not even know exist. I can swear red,
> blue and purple for twenty minutes without repeating myself once!
> And it is only my manners that are restraining me from doing so now.
> They may be rough, these manners which you dismiss with such aris-
> tocratic scorn; they may not be polished and shining and false like
> those of your careful little English world, but they were good enough
> for my mother and father, and they should be good enough for you
> too, because they come from the heart and are dictated neither by
> fashion nor snobbery. . . .

Naturally, given the literary landscape in which the play is set,
Axel is also the embodiment of vigor and freshness, a contrast to
the effete and class-conscious Europeans; and his wife, an Elliot
from Boston, surpasses the English in prudery and outraged conventionality. Type and stereotype are thus interwoven, and Coward can revel in the artificialities of a Victorian comedy while
gently poking fun at them.

The result is a love story, handled with an astringency which
makes the familiarity of it unimportant. Coward's success lies in
his handling of Serena and Axel. As with so many of Coward's
couples, and in the tradition of the comedy of manners, they are
mature people capable of being awakened to romance. And, instead of the perpetual skirmishing of somewhat bad-tempered
people who must each strive to deliver the *coup de grâce*, there is
a clash of strong temperaments who gradually achieve mutual understanding and attraction. The clash naturally demands conflict,
but in large part the conflict is between positions and points of
view, not egocentric personalities. The conflict is also relatively
free of facetiousness and insolence, no matter how elegant.

Finally, for Axel's expression of love, Coward has created a
scene which fits perfectly the tone of well-bred restraint which
dominates the play and fits Coward's own taste for sentimental
speeches which can suggest the depths of sincerity but which are
dignified on the surface, even somewhat detached from the matter

at hand. Left alone toward the end of Act II, their victory over the runaways complete, Serena and Axel consider the end of their adventure. To brush aside her feelings of anti-climax, Serena encourages Axel to tell her of his life on the railroads. This is a subject on which he is easily carried away; Serena grows more and more interested; in his peroration, Axel surpasses himself:

Oh, Lord, the whole of life seems newly washed, seen from the open door of a caboose. . . . The tail end of a freight train, the last car of all, a small shaky cabin with a twisted iron ladder climbing to the roof, that is the home of the brakeman. There he sits, hour in hour out, watching the trees marching along, and the cinders and earth and sands of America slipping away beneath the wheels. He can watch the sun set over the gentle farmlands of Wisconsin and rise over the interminable prairies of Nebraska and Illinois and Kansas. Those flat, flat lands bring the sky so low that on clear nights you can almost feel that you are rattling along through the stars. It is rougher going in the mountains where there are sharp curves and steep gradients and the locomotive strains and gasps and fills the air with steam and sparks; tunnels close round you, infernos of noise and sulphurous smoke, then suddenly you are in the open and can breathe again and there are snow-covered peaks towering above you and pine forests and the sound of waterfalls. Over it all and through it all, the familiar, reassuring noise of the train; a steady beat on the level stretches when the wheels click over the joints in the rails but changing into wilder rhythms when you clatter over bridges and intersections. The railroad is my dream, ma'am, the whole meaning of my life, my pride and all my hopes for the future—come to my country one day. Let me take you in a private car from Chicago to the West, a car specially designed by George Mortimer Pullman. The luxury of it will soothe and startle you; sofas and chairs of damask of the most violent patterns but infinitely comfortable; dark, grinning servants to wait on you; fresh iced celery from Kalamazoo. Rainbow trout from the Rocky Mountains, and outside the wide windows of your drawing-room you shall see the New World passing by. . . .

This style is not the one of *Private Lives*, although the plots have much in common, nor of *Present Laughter*; for cutting wit and jaunty irreverence are in short supply in *Quadrille*. However, this is a sign of difference rather than of inferiority. There is no falling off in the skill with which scenes flow onward; and, if smiles are more frequent than laughs, this reaction is as it should be for this more gentle comedy.

XIV   One-Acts

Before attempting to draw any general conclusions about Coward's comedy, brief consideration is due two one-act plays from *Tonight at 8:30* that do not fit any of the categories discussed above but that deserve a place in any listing of Coward's best work. *"Red Peppers"* is a kind of revue sketch framed by parodies of music hall turns, but *Fumed Oak* is Maugham's *The Bread Winner* translated into middle-class terms.

The action of *"Red Peppers"* "takes place on the stage, a dressing-room, and the stage again of the Palace of Varieties in one of the smaller English provincial towns." As the curtain opens, George and Lily Pepper are performing their "sailor" number. The number ends with "a neat walk off together, one behind the other, with their telescopes under their arms," but on this evening Lily drops her telescope and scrambles to retrieve it, thereby spoiling the whole effect. Back in their dressing-room, the Peppers begin to quarrel, eventually involving and antagonizing the orchestra conductor, the theater manager, and Mabel Grace, "a faded ex-West End actress" who performs a melodramatic one-act play on the program. At the peak of their quarreling, the call comes for their second number, a "Man About Town" routine, which ends disastrously when the conductor, to get his revenge, speeds up the tempo of their dance. Lily, in a rage, throws her hat at him, screaming, "You great drunken fool!"

This piece is appealing because of the affectionate parody of the old vaudeville routines, and because of the picture given of vigorous backstage bickering. The quarreling is also, in a sense, affectionate parody; for here are epitomized virtually all the features of the typical "peek behind the scenes": the entertainer's egotism and pride, his self-delusion and panic that success is slipping away, and, most of all, the talent for defensive bluster and insult. Both types of scene are distinguished by rapid pace and by the crackle of the lines. As is usually the case with works which Coward wrote for himself and Gertrude Lawrence, *"Red Peppers"* demands actors of versatility and timing.

Fumed Oak was also written for Coward and Miss Lawrence, but it depends a good deal less on their nervous energy. Like its ancestor, *The Bread Winner*, the play says that a lifetime of mechanical work and of arid family life is a fearful fate. Maugham's hero is a well-to-do, respectable stockbroker who is driven to recognize the emptiness of his life when he is on the verge of bankruptcy; but Coward's Henry Gow is a meek shop clerk who must save and plan for many years before he is ready to bid farewell to his shrewish wife, his crotchety mother-in-law, and his adenoidal daughter. And, whereas Maugham's play looks toward the comedy of ideas, Coward focuses on the cathartic effect of Henry Gow's final "telling off" of his family.

Fumed Oak demonstrates once again Coward's great skill in compression; like *Still Life, Ways and Means, Hands Across the Sea,* and *"Red Peppers,"* it makes one regret that he has written so few one-act plays and devoted so much of his time to full-length productions that only rarely achieve the unity of these shorter ones. The play is in two scenes: first, a breakfast scene in which Henry Gow speaks a total of five words, the rest of the lines being devoted to the wrangling among the three women. In eight pages, Coward succeeds brilliantly in establishing the atmosphere of perpetual nagging and whining in which Henry lives. Only Henry's unconcern about being late for work and the fact that he leaves without finishing his haddock suggest that he is not a totally demoralized creature.

The second scene begins with Henry's wife, Doris; his daughter, Elsie; and Mrs. Rockett, his mother-in-law, waiting to leave for the movies. But Henry, instead of meekly obeying, begins to answer back; and, in a few moments, finding how easy it is to assert himself, tells them what he thinks of them, announces that he has saved over five hundred pounds, and then departs, with a pseudonym on his passport, for exotic shores. The best comment on this scene is in a brief exchange between husband and wife:

> Doris: A fine exhibition you're making of yourself, I must say.
> Henry: Not bad, is it? As a matter of fact I'm rather pleased with it myself.

Nor can the audience fail to enjoy it, so carefully has Coward stacked the cards.

In its preoccupations, *Fumed Oak* is quite unlike Coward's other comedies. Pictures of domestic life, particularly that of the middle-class, have occupied his attention in serious plays; but in his comedies Coward has remained faithful to a narrow stratum of society, the very well-to-do, be they aristocrats, businessmen or successful painters, writers or actors. There is some concern about money in *I'll Leave It to You*, *Nude with Violin*, *Ways and Means* and the early part of *Design for Living*; but, even when such concern may be prominent, there is virtually no sense of desperation, of scrimping and saving, such as there is in *Fumed Oak*. Despite this difference, however, *Fumed Oak* is a true member of Coward's canon, for it draws heavily on one of his chief talents—that for insult.

XV *Assessment*

Discussions of comedy reveal that the variety of definitions and descriptions equals and very likely surpasses the variety of those applied to tragedy. Through all the discussions, however, a few ideas reappear persistently; and, though none applies equally well to all comedies, each seems to apply very well to some. One of these ideas is that comedy appeals to and flatters the viewers' sense of superiority. Basically, the argument contends that the viewers are amused and entertained by a pratfall because they feel themselves secure, superior, and even smug in their security.

In the case of high comedy, where pratfalls are rare, the audience shares with the witty people the superiority they enjoy over the fools or even, in a battle of wits, over one another. Sometimes, as in high farces like Wilde's *The Importance of Being Earnest*, both kinds of superiority may be involved; while aware of the ludicrousness of the situations and characters as a whole, the audience can also, once the new logic has been established, share in the characters' wit, particularly in the battle of wit. Of the many theories applied to comedy, this one certainly fits Coward best. Those discussions which treat of comedy as a form of social therapy, a theory that beautifully fits plays like Molière's *The Misanthrope*, or those that find the comic rhythm one of rebirth and renewal, as in Shakespeare's *Twelfth Night*, can be applied to Coward's work only by extreme ingenuity.

In *Fumed Oak*, as stated above, the cards are stacked. Henry Gow's family is so utterly repulsive that not for a moment can the audience feel anything but delight at their comeuppance. *Nude with Violin* has another such black and white arrangement; but, on the whole, Coward is less obvious, sometimes veering toward a sharp division between the clever and the foolish, as in *Hay Fever,* and sometimes concentrating on the duel between equals, as in *Private Lives.* What is distinctive about Coward's comedy is the extent to which superiority depends not so much on greater sensibleness or on more realistic or perceptive ethics, nor on the ability to turn a phrase, but on a talent for vituperation and insolence.

This distinctiveness is a matter of content even more than one of style. Aside from Sebastien's speeches on the spuriousness of modern art, Garry Essendine's defense of his own hedonism and his attacks on hypocrisy, and the assorted comments on success in *Design for Living,* Coward's comedies are virtually devoid of ideas or serious satire. He of course deflates hypocrites and scorns stuffy and unrealistic conventionality, but his hypocrites and prudes are usually cardboard figures. As for adultery, which plays such a large part in almost all the comedies, it is taken for granted that, after a certain period, usually three years, passion cools and a new attraction is inevitable and justified, especially when the rejected spouse is dull. Most of the comedies deal with the obstacles to a strenuous hedonism; as a result, they mainly consist of skirmishing in which sophisticates are confronted by their inferiors and resort consciously or automatically to insolence and rudeness, or sophisticates confront each other and trade insults.

What saves the best comedies from the cruelty implicit in many of the situations and from the banality of ideas is Coward's theatrical skill and his real, if specialized, wit. His skill is mainly a matter of preparation. Reviewers frequently comment on the slow first acts in Coward's plays, but the thorough exposition of the first act serves as a contrast to the rapidly increasing tempo of the next acts and, even more important, prepares the foundation of character and situation on which the latter parts of the play stand. This technique is more than Ibsenite thoroughness; for, as noted frequently, the heart of any Coward comedy is in the second act. And these second acts are frequently duologues—seductions, quarrels, drunk scenes—which may do little to make the plot progress but are, as it were, cadenzas with an air of spontaneity and elegant variation. Without careful introduction of character and situation, the cadenzas would hardly be possible.

Coward's method is most successful when the theme is simple

and the exposition can be expedited. *Private Lives,* which demonstrates this success, has a first act that is largely expository, in preparation for the long scene of love play and quarreling which occupies the second act; but the exposition is neither solemn nor tedious. The paralleling of scenes between Elyot and his wife and between Amanda and her husband serves to provide all the needed information; and they are also comic in themselves. When Elyot and Amanda meet again, they are able to move forward with the narrative; there is no need for additional explanation. In *Present Laughter,* Coward resorts to an even older expedient, the stranger to whom background must be explained. Sometimes, as in *Hay Fever* or *Blithe Spirit,* the exposition is so obvious that only the briskness with which it is carried forward and the clearly implied attitude that some information must be gotten out of the way before the play can begin can save appearances. Whatever the method, however, Coward learned early that at least a semblance of realistic logic must support his *jeux d'esprits.*

In a less obvious way, even those moments which convey the fullest sense of spontaneity and playfulness reveal a solidity of construction. Critics have been too easily misled by Coward's admissions of speed in writing (*Private Lives,* for example, took a mere five days to put on paper) and by the brilliance of performance; and they have concluded that the writing is the least part of it. If a successful play of Coward's suggests that he had dictated from his bath "bits and pieces of dialogue which a secretary took down in the intervals of turning on the gramophone and mixing a drink," [12] the impression need not be taken for the truth.

Clever repetition is also a prominent technique, as in the second act of *Private Lives,* where Elyot and Amanda, relaxing after dinner, engage in random badinage which eventually culminates in a violent quarrel. The scene begins with whimsical small talk:

Amanda: I'm glad we let Louise go. I am afraid she is going to have a cold.
Elyot: Going to have a cold; she's been grunting and snorting all the evening like a whole herd of Bison.
Amanda [*thoughtfully*]: Bison never sounds right to me somehow. I have a feeling it ought to be Bisons, a flock of Bisons.
Elyot: You might say a covey of Bisons, or even a school of Bisons.
Amanda: Yes, lovely. The Royal London School of Bisons.

In a few moments, however, a trace of seriousness becomes evident in the conversation, and with it a hint of bad temper and nagging:

Amanda: We sent Victor and Sibyl a nice note from wherever it was, what more can they want?
Elyot: You're even more ruthless than I am.
Amanda: I don't believe in crying over my bridge before I've eaten it.
Elyot: Very sensible.
Amanda: Personally I feel grateful for a miraculous escape. I know now that I should never have been happy with Victor. I was a fool ever to consider it.
Elyot: You did a little more than consider it.
Amanda: Well, you can't talk.

And in another two minutes, having solemnly sworn to say "Sollocks" whenever a quarrel is imminent, they have plunged into a squabble about Claire Lavenham, and a pattern is established: badinage and love-talk alternate with increasingly dangerous reminiscence and insult; and, each time a return is made to small talk, a larger residue of temper is left to smolder. Brief excerpts suggest that the scene consists of bits and pieces, but actually the whole is relentlessly organized. Even the phone call is most carefully timed, coming at a moment when passion is about to brush aside all other considerations. Its effect is once more to remind them of their situation, and the pattern of reassurance, leading to reminiscence, which in turn leads to recrimination, is reestablished. Although the final fist fight is ignited by a triviality, it has become inevitable. The last act, in which Victor and Sibyl repeat the quarrel in their terms while Elyot and Amanda sneak off, places the whole play within a symmetrical frame which is yet another form of repetition.

Design for Living, Hay Fever, Nude with Violin, Quadrille, and "*Red Peppers*" are other obvious cases in which clever or elegant variation within a symmetrical form is not only the chief principle of construction but implicitly the meaning of the play. The parallels between opening and closing scenes stress the absence of significant change, emphasize the artificiality of what has been only a game. The exposition outlines the characters and indicates the type of situation in which they are most apt to find themselves, and then the rest of the play "develops" this material, but not in the usual sense of exhibiting the characters in the process of growth and change. Instead, a Coward play develops as a photograph is developed: an initial impression is clarified and fixed.

Skill in construction is not, of course, what mainly concerns the readers or the audiences of a Coward comedy. Laughter is what they want, and that is what they usually get. The sources of that laughter, like the construction materials, are surprisingly limited. Much of it comes from the incongruities of situation (the mistress in the bedroom while the wife chats in the living room; the pompous clergyman mistaking the mistress for the wife; Judith Bliss wearing galoshes with a tea gown; the spirit of the first wife invisible and inaudible to the second); some of the best comes from carefully observed and/or created comic types—like Mrs. Rockett, the epitome of the comic strip mother-in-law in *Fumed Oak*, or Madame Arcati, the hearty spiritualist in *Blithe Spirit*— but most from the acidulated speech of the sophisticated.

As Maugham has aptly pointed out, one difference between Coward's style and that of the comic playwrights who preceded him is that his dialogue is much more naturalistic. There is very little of the epigrammatic, previously so fashionable; Maugham claims that "when an early play of mine, *Lady Frederick*, was bought by Mr. George Tyler, he told me that it was not epigrammatic enough, so I went away and in two hours wrote in twenty-four." Maugham is referring to that form of naturalism which presents people who "do talk grammatically, do choose their words, and do make use of expressions that on the stage would be thought 'bookish.'" [13] A good example of such dialogue is the following from *Present Laughter*:

Garry: You're predatory as hell! . . . You got the wretched Hugo when he was convalescent, you've made a dead set at Morris, and now, by God, you're after me! Don't deny it—I can see it in your eye. You suddenly appear out of the night reeking with the lust of conquest, the whole atmosphere's quivering with it! You had your hair done this afternoon, didn't you? And your nails and probably your feet too! You've never worn those stockings before in your life! And your mind, even more expertly groomed to vanquish than your body. Every word, every phrase, every change of mood cunningly planned. Just the right amount of sex antagonism mixed with subtle flattery, just the right switch over, perfectly timed, from provocative implication to wistful diffidence. You want to know what I'm really like, do you, under all the glittering veneer? Well, this is it. This is what I'm really like— fundamentally honest! When I'm driven into a corner I tell the truth, and the truth at the moment is that I know you, Joanna, I know what you're after, I can see through every trick. Go away from me! Leave me alone!

This speech certainly contains no jokes or word play. It is hard to imagine an audience laughing at any particular point, and in a more serious context it might just possibly be taken quite seriously. Yet, it is comic, and context is only part of it. Even more important is that the speaker himself appreciates, indeed relishes, his articulateness and the perception it reveals. We delight with him, and with the author, in the use of hyperbole ("reeking with the lust of conquest"); that is not just *le mot juste* but *le mot juste* with bells on—and other examples abound. Sometimes it is not so much hyperbole that speaker and audience relish but the oblique, brightly irrelevant. Here is Serena in *Quadrille* talking about one of her husband's earlier mistresses: "She was the widow of an Indian colonel. Hubert was devoted to her for nearly two years. She died ultimately in Harrogate and left him a set of Benares brass-ware, a large luncheon gong and a musical box that played three tunes and had a picture of Loch Lomond inside the lid. I am afraid we still have it somewhere." Sometimes it is from the delight in verbal embroidery, as in this quotation from *Hay Fever*.

Judith: I'm much more dignified on the stage than in the country— it's my milieu. I've tried terribly hard to be "landed gentry," but without any real success. I long for excitement and glamour. Think of the thrill of a first night; all those ardent playgoers willing one to succeed; the critics all leaning forward with glowing faces, receptive and exultant—emitting queer little inarticulate noises as some witty line tickles their fancy. The satisfied grunt of the Daily Mail, the abandoned gurgle of the Sunday Times, and the shrill enthusiastic scream of the Daily Express! I can distinguish them all.

Even when a character is being serious, there is an undercurrent of this same delight in the choice of words and example. One of the surest signs of a character's inferiority in a Coward comedy is that he speaks unself-consciously in clichés and does not or cannot dramatize himself and his feelings, cannot participate in the verbal battle, and does not sense the pleasure of saying things brightly to silence an opponent.

It is in the give and take of dialogue that the full effect of such comedy can be appreciated:

Garry: The thing that astonishes me in life is people's arrogance! It's fantastic. Look at you all! Gossiping in corners, whispering behind your fans, telling me what to do and what not to do. . . . What happens if I relax my loving hold on any of you for a minute? Disaster! I happen to go to New York to play a three months' season. Hugo immediately gets pneumonia, goes to Biarritz to recover, meets Joanna and marries her! I go away for a brief holiday to San Tropez for a month in 1937, and when I come back what do I find? You and Morris between you have bought the dullest Hungarian play ever written and put it into rehearsal with Phoebe Lucas in the leading part. Phoebe Lucas, playing a glamorous courtesan with about as much sex appeal as a haddock! How long did it run? One week! And that was only because the press said it was lascivious.

Liz: Isn't all this a little beside the point?

Garry: Certainly not. Twenty years ago Hugo put all his money into *The Lost Cavalier*. And who played it for eighteen months to capacity with extra matinees? And who started his whole career as a producer in that play? Morris!

Liz: I wish you'd stop asking questions and answering them yourself, it's making me giddy.

Garry: Where would they have been without me? Where would Monica be now if I hadn't snatched her away from that sinister old aunt of hers and given her a job?

Liz: With the sinister old aunt.

Garry: And you! One of the most depressing, melancholy actresses on the English stage. Where would you be if I hadn't forced you to give up acting and start writing?

Liz: Regent's Park.

. . . . .

Liz: You're just as dependent on us anyway now. We stop you being extravagant and buying houses every five minutes. We stopped you in the nick of time from playing Peer Gynt.

Garry: I still maintain I should have been magnificent as Peer Gynt.

Liz: Above all, we stop you from overacting.

Garry: You have now gone too far, Liz. I think you had better go away somewhere.

Liz: I've only just come back.

Garry [*shouting*]: Monica! Monica! Come here at once.

Monica [*entering*]: What on earth's the matter?

Garry: Have you or have you not ever seen me overact?

Monica: Frequently.

Garry: It's a conspiracy! I knew it!

Monica: As a matter of fact you're overacting now. [*She goes off.*]

Garry: Very well, I give in. Everybody's against me. It doesn't matter about me—oh no—I'm only the breadwinner. It doesn't matter how much I'm wounded and insulted! It doesn't matter that my timorous belief in myself should be subtly undermined.

Liz: Your belief in yourself is about as timorous as Napoleon's.

Garry: And look what happened to him. He died forsaken and alone on a beastly little island in the middle of the sea.

Liz: Islands have that in common.

In this prototypical Coward scene, each character is delightedly playing a role; Liz is clearly enjoying her crisp, disingenuous statements as much as Garry does his rhetorical questions and his choice of adjectives. And how well the scene is contrived to give full weight to Monica's laconic, "Frequently." Throughout there is the tension created by sharp-witted people ready to pounce on one another's errors, exaggerations, or clichés. When Coward is at his best—when situation, character and tempo are successfully merged—the effect can be exhilarating.

CHAPTER 5

Off Stage

THE most persistent refrain running through all the criticism about Coward is the phrase "a man of the theatre," and how completely deserved this title is should be clear at this point. Yet, there is even more evidence which should be added to the three chapters above: (1) Coward's work with the films as actor, writer, and director; (2) his work on television; and (3) his intermittent but highly successful career as a solo entertainer at military installations, in concert halls, cafés, and night clubs. He has even had one brief flirtation with ballet, providing the scenario and music for a ballet entitled *London Morning*, presented by the London Festival Ballet in 1959. His versatility and capacity for hard work have not only resulted in more than fifty works for the stage, but made it possible for him to appear in many of them and to direct most of them. He has appeared in and has directed plays by other playwrights. He has also contributed songs, sketches, and other materials to revues in which he took no other part.

But this list is not a complete one of his works, for he has also found time to publish three volumes of satires (primarily parodies), three volumes of autobiography, a volume of talks given in Australia during World War II, three collections of short stories, and one novel, plus a number of pieces, both fiction and non-fiction, which have as yet appeared only in periodicals. As a whole, these works, of considerably lesser importance than his plays, demonstrate once more Coward's great versatility and productivity.

I *Autobiography*

The three autobiographical volumes are *Present Indicative* (1937), *Future Indefinite* (1954), and *Middle East Diary* (1944). The first two are in the standard autobiographical mode; for

Present Indicative covers Coward's life from birth to October, 1931, and *Future Indefinite* deals with the period from 1939 through 1945. *Middle East Diary* is an account of three months spent during the summer of 1943 entertaining troops and visitin᾿ hospitals in Malta and in Cairo, Beirut, and other areas in th Middle East.

Coward expresses his annoyance with the public that insists seeing him always as "this publicised sybarite, this mannered e otic, flicking the useless froth of society from his blue pin stripe"; [1] and the relative lifelessness of these volumes is probably a result of his concern to alter this impression. He concentrates on straight reporting in a generally formal and flat tone that is here and there decorated with strained and purplish diction which he would be the first to ridicule in a stage bore.

The figure of Coward that emerges from his autobiographies is not that of "the talented, neurotic, sophisticated playboy," but a person who is no more attractive and a good deal less interesting. If the "Noel, dahrrling" that is the mimic's stock in trade looks at the world with a jaded disdain that is at once enviable and a convenient target for laughter, the Noel Coward of *Present Indicative, Future Indefinite,* and even *Middle East Dairy* is merely and unimaginatively egocentric. He records clearly what he does, where he goes, what he sees, and what he feels about his own situation; but he rarely stops to reflect on anything more significant than his own momentary role. Coward apparently conceives his autobiographies to be accounts, not analyses, of his experiences; feels that his inner life is not for publication; and that, since there are ample histories to cover the larger movements of his time, he is responsible only for that narrow band of information which is left. The result is a supplement to Coward's main work but one of very little intrinsic interest.

II *Parodies*

The parodies date from the earliest years of Coward's writing, and the first collection *A Withered Nosegay* (in America, with some addition, *Terribly Intimate Portraits*) appeared in 1922. *Chelsea Buns* was published in 1925, and *Spangled Unicorn,* primarily a compilation of the two earlier collections, was published in 1932. It is not very surprising that, coming from such a young

man, they should be sophomoric and repetitious. The level of satiric writing is well represented by this "beautiful little lullaby of
Herman Viegel's":

> Baby white and baby red,
>   Like a moon convulsive,
> Rolling up and down the bed,
>   Utterly repulsive!

Very rarely is there anything as good as this description of Anna
Podd, mistress of the Tsar: "She was wont to sway rhythmically
and sinuously to the crazy band which played for her; now and
then, with pain in her heart and a merry laugh on her lips, she
would leap onto the tables and snap her fingers indiscriminately."
On the whole, the general effect of the parodies is, as in Coward's
earliest comedies, of an author straining vainly after comic effect
through facetiousness.

III   *Short Stories*

In Coward's short stories there are flashes of satirical comment
and a lightly ironic edge, somewhat in the manner of Maugham;
but few are comic. In his stories even more than in his plays,
Coward is a traditionalist. The stories echo the solid, Edwardian
fiction of Arnold Bennett or John Galsworthy. The subjects are
frequently drawn, unsurprisingly, from the milieu of the theater
or Society, but there is little of the sprightliness and nervous energy that buoy up the plays. There is a four-square, formal thoroughness about the writing.

There is always very careful attention to details: the names of
streets, the location of theaters and restaurants, the furnishings of
hotel rooms, the appropriate brands of cigarettes and liquors, and
the names and idiosyncrasies of the means of transportation. The
same thoroughness is applied to the main characters, who are
usually provided with a concise biography and a list of salient
traits. The stories have a professional glossiness but few if any
clues that would help a reader identify most of them as Coward's
work.

None of the stories is more than a poignant, pathetic or comic
anecdote. In the most successful, *What Mad Pursuit?*, the protag-

onist is Evan Lorrimer, a successful, highly respected English novelist who agrees to undertake a lecture tour in the United States. Although an amiable and adaptable person, he does have one problem: without at least eight hours of uninterrupted sleep each day, "his whole organism disintegrated." After the first hectic days in New York, he gladly accepts an invitation to spend the weekend with the Steinhausers at the Long Island home where, he is promised, he will find nothing but "peace and good food."

Sunday becomes, however, a nightmare of cocktail parties, meals with thirty or forty guests, long rides in crowded cars over icy roads, and finally, a room shortage that results in Evan's sharing a room with his host, who snores. Only one remedy remains; Evan dresses, sneaks out of the house, walks to the nearest village, catches a train back to New York, and catches up on his sleep in his hotel room. Unlike many of his other stories, *What Mad Pursuit?* is largely told through dialogue; and the conversations have much of the sparkle of Coward's best comedies.

IV   Pomp and Circumstance

Noel Coward's talents as a writer of fiction came to a full flowering in 1960 with *Pomp and Circumstance*. It was Coward's first published novel, although the autobiographies indicate a number of previous, abortive attempts to write one. The narrator of *Pomp and Circumstance* is Grizelda Craigie, wife of an English planter on the island of Samola. In her forties, Grizelda is intelligent, witty, and at once warm-hearted and jaundiced in her outlook. In other words, she is the very embodiment of Coward's comic spirit.

The story is an interweaving of farcical plots, one group having to do with the forthcoming visit of the Queen and Prince Phillip, the other concerning the amorous intrigue of Bunny Colville and Eloise, Duchess of Fowey. Neither subject, however, prevents Coward from practicing his talent for witty conversations and comic scenes which may have little or nothing to do with the progress of the story.

Pomp and Circumstance is, therefore, very much in the line of the high farces, where the most improbable events fail to diminish the characters' aplomb. Grizelda's most frequent statement is "I'll explain later," and each time it follows on a series of misunderstandings of circumstantial complications and involved relationships, which are at once logical but almost impossible to summarize. And, as in the high farces, nothing stimulates the characters' wit more than a crisis.

The loose form of the novel and the voluble nature of his narrator allow Coward more opportunity than his short stories or plays for passages of a generally philosophical nature; and nowhere else, not even in the autobiographies, has Coward spoken at such length about such subjects as love and ethics. The speaker in the following passage is Grizelda, and she echoes what her creator has touched on in many places:

Personally I cling to no . . . ambiguous hopes. I have very definite feelings about an afterlife, and they are nearly all on the debit side. I find it difficult enough in this brief span to cope successfully with old friends who suddenly appear from the long ago, changed beyond all recognition and expecting that our relationship should be resumed on the same terms that it was before, quite regardless of the disrupting years between. The thought that immediately the last breath has left my body I shall be transported lock, stock, and barrel onto some nameless celestial plane and plumped down among a crowd of old chums whom I haven't thought of for years, fills me with dismay. Also, I do believe that when the time comes for me to die, providing I don't get bashed to death in an aeroplane or drowned or written off in some violent accident, that I shall be ready for it and reconciled to it. I envisage myself as . . . very old . . . with a certain wistful pleasure. I shall try my best not to be a nuisance to other people, although I am sure I shall snap a bit at moments just to keep my hand in . . . I may become a fractious old monster, deaf as a post and full of wind and ghastliness, or I might pack up, embittered and lonely and very cross indeed, in some awful boardinghouse in Folkestone. There is no knowing really, and it really isn't any good worrying about it or making plans. One must just face up to it when it does come, and square one's frail bent shoulders and try to be as dignified as possible.

Since *Pomp and Circumstance* is such a fictional vaudeville, there is room for almost any topic to be touched on; and Coward manages to throw some well-aimed darts at, among other things, currently fashionable literature and its devotees; English class distinctions; the "romance" of tropical climes and, particularly, American women's magazines, with their preposterous recipes and their impossibly high standards of home decorating and management.

Pomp and Circumstance and *What Mad Pursuit?* are Noel Coward's most successful works of fiction. Both are comic extravaganzas paralleling such stage works as *Hay Fever* and *Blithe Spirit.* Coward's short stories and his one novel are small, glittering pendants attached to his work as a playwright.

CHAPTER 6

Present Mirth and Present Laughter

NOEL COWARD was born in 1899, twenty years after Nora Helmer slammed the front door of Ibsen's doll's house and provided literary historians with a convenient point to label the start of modern drama, indeed the start of modern literature. Like all such neat formulations, this one contains at best only a half-truth; but, in this case a very important one: namely, that the characteristically modern writer has felt himself to be at the very least a critic examining society's weaknesses or an agonized witness to the convulsions of the twentieth century, and often a physician diagnosing and prescribing for mankind's ills. Often, whether the writer has been dealing with social or esthetic matters, he has felt compelled, like Nora, to say "No"; he has felt committed to condemning the old, lying ways and searching for a new way to live and write truthfully.

The artists of Coward's generation (for example, Aldous Huxley and J. B. Priestley, both born in 1894; Robert Graves, 1895; and Evelyn Waugh and George Orwell, 1903) have almost all in some way or other shared this attitude. Few writers in the 1920's and 1930's, when Coward was so busy laying the foundations of his work, believed it was either possible or desirable to be non-political, disengaged.

But Coward is totally apart from his contemporaries. He has been working steadily for over fifty years, during a period which has witnessed some of the most staggering and violent changes in society, in politics, in science, in every aspect of life. Out of a total of more than fifty titles, only a handful reveal, however, any trace of the world outside an extremely limited and artificial milieu. And even those few works are rather special, for in most of them, *Cavalcade* and *This Happy Breed,* for example, crucial events of the last half century are presented as nostalgic souvenirs, not as items for deep concern: the Boer War, the death of Queen Victoria, the General Strike and the abdication of Edward VIII are all given the same glaze of sentiment, the same sense of "Remember? Remember when . . . ?" Even the autobiographies provide little comment on anything outside Coward's own immediate concerns, and those concerns are almost always connected with the theater.

During World War II, Coward emerged as a deeply sentimental patriot in *This Happy Breed,* both play and film; in the original film, *In Which We Serve;* in a number of comic songs, notably "Don't Let's Be Beastly to the Germans"; and in a popular poem, "Lie in the Dark and Listen." None of these, his most "engaged" work, deal with anything but the most obvious, most theatrical aspects of a situation. "Lie in the Dark and Listen" (1943) presents in brief form both the virtues and weaknesses of Coward's most serious response to the world around him; and the first stanza of the poem illustrates these characteristics:

> Lie in the dark and listen.
> It's clear tonight, so they're flying high,
> Hundreds of them, thousands perhaps,
> Riding the icy, moonlit sky,
> Men, machinery, bombs and maps,
> Altimeters and guns and charts,
> Coffee, sandwiches, fleece-lined boots,
> Bones and muscles and minds and hearts,
> English saplings with English roots
> Deep in the earth they've left below.
> Lie in the dark and let them go;
> Lie in the dark and listen.

Aside from its strong rhythmic flow and rhyming, both of which owe a good deal to Coward's many years of song writing, this poem is perhaps most admirble for the smooth way it combines cinematic images with straight preaching in a direct appeal to the reader's emotion and patriotism. The whole poem is a rhymed scenario for a film of strong contrasts—heroic pilots and puny civilians, sharp silhouettes of bombers crossing the moon and tawdry nightclubs—with light or pathetic realistic touches, the whole done with verve and style; but it is no more profound than a hundred other films or plays.

And yet, how basically unsatisfactory the poem is—how cliché-ridden, how it seems to calculate its effects. What has become of

the Noel Coward who had previously had at least some inklings of
the horrors of war, its ugliness and wastefulness? What has become of the Noel Coward who had a sharp ear for the pompous
cliché and the strained metaphor? Although Coward is the very
picture of sophisticated insolence and amorality in his comedies
and in his usual public role, he, when his attention turns to national concerns, reveals himself as the spokesman for the bourgeois values, the ones usually glorified in the mass entertainment
media.

The most serious attempt to place Coward in the mainstream of
twentieth-century thought was made, significantly enough, in the
early 1930's. When critic Frank Swinnerton in *The Georgian
Scene,* attempted to cover in some detail the history of English
letters from 1910 to 1934, Coward was grouped with Aldous
Huxley, Richard Aldington, and Wyndham Lewis in a chapter
entitled "Post-War Pessimism." The work of these four is, according to Mr. Swinnerton, "a direct outcome of the mood of dissatis-
faction, even despair, by which honest and thoughtful young people were seized as they saw the consequences of four years of
slaughter." [1] Mr. Swinnerton says that Coward's plays "are among
the most moral plays ever written," a point he does not discuss
further; and he concludes from Coward's defense of *Design for
Living* that "one can tell from this protest that Coward, though a
writer supposedly frivolous, has a serious purpose. It is his object
to mirror contemporary life. Not all contemporary life, but a section of it. And the part he mirrors is a part given to promiscuity,
drunkenness, drugging, and fighting." [2]

Mr. Swinnerton concludes that Coward's "quality lies in his fun.
He has great sense of the stage"; but, when his characters "are the
mouthpieces of Coward's morality, my heart sinks": "I grow un-
comfortable, not because (like the massed illiteracy of the Middle
Classes) I am shocked, but merely because I have heard smart
sentimentalists who begin with 'I mean' and who think in the
clichés of their day talk just like that. . . ." [3]

In what way, then, does Coward deserve consideration in a
chapter devoted to those who "feel that the world is a revolting
place, and a hopeless place," who "all want to do as Omar
Khayyam wanted to do so long ago, and smash the world to bits
so as to remould it nearer to the heart's desire."? [4] Mr. Swinnerton
seems actually to be looking ahead, expecting Coward to recog-

nize the narrowness of his concerns and to dramatize the feelings and ideas which are presumed to underlie the fun and the theatrical fireworks. It was not to be, and even such limited rebelliousness and healthy frankness as Swinnerton recognized in *Design for Living* (1933) had just about made their last appearance in that play.

Mr. Swinnerton was not, however, the only critic to find depth and significance in Coward's work. At least until the end of World War II, most writers dealing with Coward felt that there lay beneath the surface a foundation of critical attitudes that gave meaning to the whole. Only in recent years—particularly since writers like John Osborne and Arnold Wesker have given the intellectual a new value in the English theater—have some flatly denied this quality: "What on earth, you wonder . . . what on earth is all this *about?* . . . When he is at his most serious he is most inconsequent. What, for example, are we to make of *The Vortex?* What is Florence's motivation—or Nicky's? The play abounds in 'theatrical' lines, lines which are really meaningless but which sound immensely effective within the strict unliterary, unthinking conventions of the classic West End theatre." [5]

However, Coward is primarily a writer of comedy; and very few writers of comedy have been successful with non-comic plays (Shakespeare is the only one that comes readily to mind). Furthermore, comic writers from Aristophanes on have been notoriously conservative, Bernard Shaw being one of the few exceptions. Finally, again excepting Shaw, what comic writers, as distinct from satirists, have made contemporary political or social issues part of their theater at all? In his major plays Congreve was concerned about fortune-hunters, tyrannical guardians, stupid country bumpkins, dandies, fops, would-be wits, and true wits; but one would be hard pressed to determine from Congreve's plays what party was in power or what issues were most puzzling members of Parliament. Even plain-spoken, bad-tempered Wycherley was for the most part speaking plainly about sexual immorality and venting his ire against hypocrisy, neither a particularly original nor specifically contemporary topic. Thus, any evaluation of Coward must allow for this inherent conservatism of comedy and must recognize his apolitical views. His plays must be examined apart from the twentieth-century demand for contemporaneity and involvement.

I *Neither Rebel nor Reactionary*

At once, paradox presents itself. If Coward is speaking seriously, he is rarely more up-to-date than the retired colonel still living in his memories of the White Raj, nor more critical of society than the latest Walt Disney "family" movie, Coward speaking comically and apparently about nothing at all remains brightly and smartly contemporary. For at least the first fifteen years of his career, Coward's critics were most concerned about encouraging him to use his talents in coming to grips with the world around him and in suggesting, some gently, some brutally, that all this other trivia that he produced so easily was doomed to swift oblivion.

Nor has this pattern entirely changed; writing in 1953, J. C. Trewin is willing to suggest that *Hay Fever* (1925), *Private Lives* (1930), and *Blithe Spirit* (1941) "would survive in a hundred years as representative period pieces" and even now demonstrate "how little the essential Coward has altered." But Trewin can blandly predict of *Relative Values* (1951) that "this comedy will look very queer in the cold print of some collected edition twenty-five years on." [6] This statement sounds embarrassingly like Ivor Brown's 1930 prediction that "within a few years the student of drama will be sitting in complete bewilderment before the text of *Private Lives.*"

If Mr. Trewin's prediction turns out to be more accurate than Mr. Brown's, it will be so because *Relative Values* is in some way inferior to the three he praises, not because it is any more trivial or any more old-fashioned than they. On the contrary, Coward's comedies have been old-fashioned from the moment of their birth, still reflecting the techniques he learned so well in the 1920's, and changing little in either technique or basic philosophy since then; yet, they have not only out-lasted most of his own serious works but also a number of avant-garde movements and many "important" works by others; and it appears as if his plays will be around for quite a long time.

A Coward play has always been highly theatrical and glossily professional. We know that the dramatist feels the spot-light full upon him as he lifts his pen—as he flourishes it in a manner familiar only on the stage where any actor can write a long letter in twenty seconds and sign his name with a single dab.

Is this unfair to the most versatile theatre-man of our time and a writer with a spraying fountain (or fountain-pen) wit? I do not think so. Coward, whether as dramatist or composer, has worked invariably for the passing moment, for the present laughter rather than the applause of posterity. . . . Whatever he does, the effect is theatrical, grease-painted. First of all, he is a dramatist who writes to be acted. He is thinking of the listener and watcher, the curtain-rise, the sharp impact, the rapid effect. . . . Too often the dialogue comes thinly to the printed text. . . . Of the play as acted in the theatre, only a dim shape remains. . . .[7]

Yes, the "whacking good part" and the curtain calls have certainly been among Coward's chief criteria for his own plays, although it is important to stress once more that Mr. Trewin, like so many others, underestimates the printed text.

But can skill and theatrical flair be enough? Is Coward doomed to the fate of Dion Boucicault and Tom Taylor, two of the most "glossily professional" playwrights of the nineteenth century whose fame barely lasted their own lifetimes? Ironically enough, the skill that could do little to preserve any of Taylor's or Boucicault's plays not only has been important in keeping many of Coward's plays alive but may well preserve them quite a bit longer for the simple reason that such gloss and theatrical skill have been in rather short supply in the twentieth century. Ibsen and Chekov in their different ways set high standards of construction and polish for the modern dramatist, but they demanded that construction and polish conceal themselves. The play must be transparent, like the fourth wall, allowing us to see through it to the heart of the characters and the heart of their problems. On the other hand, the symbolists and experimenters, whose father is Strindberg, have moved in the opposite direction, drawing upon the resources of lighting, music, set design, dance, and all other theatrical devices in an effort to go beyond the narrow limitations of realism. Yet, in its own way non-realistic drama has also ignored or concealed the pure, almost child-like pleasure in exhibitionism that is so crucial to Coward's dramaturgy.

Thus, *Hay Fever* is not only one of Coward's most successful works but is virtually the prototype of all his comedies. The

Blisses, rapidly shifting roles, always on the lookout for ways to deflate each other and sharing with the audience a contempt for the poor inflexible dolts who are not up to the competition are all four Noel Cowards; unless we can share in the Blisses' fun (which is of course the playwright's fun, too), the play becomes at best mere foolishness. Much the same can be said of *Private Lives, Present Laughter,* "*Red Peppers*" and at least the major scenes from most of the other comedies. In the more serious plays, this appeal to the audience's pleasure in watching the clever show-off is only slightly masked; crucial scenes almost always involve haranguing that the audience can revel in. In *Peace in Our Time,* for example, at least half of the eight scenes depend on one of the good characters "telling off" one of the bad ones.

However, the pleasures of glossy professionalism are only part of Coward's appeal. Another part of the answer lies in the fantasy world Coward has created, a world whose appeal has, if anything, increased during this century. In his world elegance, ease, and irresponsibility are the very birthright of the splendid people who live there. Jon Whiting puts this very well when he asks that Coward write what he calls a "court play": "I mean a play designed to be performed before the very best people, such as myself and my friends, not more than two hundred of us in all. It should be given one performance, and published in a limited edition of fifteen copies. The loudest sound in any of its three acts should be the shutting of a door. The characters should be enormously rich, appallingly idle, and titled to a man. The setting should be a garden or a deserted ballroom." [8] The situations and conversation of the characters would continually remind us of how very superior we all are to the silly, hobbling strictures of bourgeois morality, but true love would triumph. It is just this compound of nose-thumbing and sentimentality, presented in the equivalent of "a garden or a deserted ballroom," which all the wit, the theatricality, and the professionalism serve. It is at once Coward's chief asset and liability.

The paradox that appeared inherent when the comedies and serious plays were compared is largely resolved. To put the resolution most simply, the comedies show Coward as the witty rebel against middle-class rigidity; but he is a safe rebel, one not inconsistent with the sentimentalist of the serious plays. Modern society has long since come to accept the proposition that each generation works its way through a period when monogamy seems one of the most foolish practices ever imposed on mankind, only to recognize, after all, the basic value of marriage. A challenge to the accepted and still basically unshaken value of love and marriage is one way to be daring, outspoken and modern; and so long as the challenge does not go very far—in fact, it generally ends by affirming the conventional values or, at the most, by suggesting that a little graceful philandering is one of the privileges of the witty and elegant—the audience will be able to share in the glow of skepticism and sophistication without making any intellectual adjustment at all.

It is significant that in only one play, *Design for Living*, does Coward create a truly unstereotyped moral problem. When the play was attacked on moral grounds, Coward turned defensive in a typically modern way:

I do resent very deeply, on my own behalf and on the behalf of those young writers who are sincerely attempting to mirror contemporary life honestly and truthfully, . . . that this weight of bourgeois ignorance and false sentimentality should not only be allowed to force those in authority to crush down rising talent for the sole reason that its outlook doesn't quite conform with the moral traditions of twenty-five years ago, but that it should be encouraged in every possible way by the Press.[9]

Yet Coward never tried to "mirror contemporary life" in any such unusual way again. Even Maugham, in so many ways Coward's model, generally gave his comedies more intellectual weight, and lost thereby in gaining continuing popularity; now that divorce is so common and acceptable, *The Circle* seems much more than forty-five years old, and a good deal of the force behind *The Constant Wife* is muted because the working wife is now such a common figure in every class of society. But Coward's more general and less serious theme, in effect asking for little more than that differences be recognized and the moral code applied accordingly, is far less dated. Although he echoes the anti-Puritanism and moral relativism that constituted something of a revolution during the 1920's, Coward remains a contemporary spokesman because his attitude has become a fixed part of twentieth-century thinking. What the audience found rather deliciously daring and wittily cynical in the comedies of 1925, it still finds so in the comedies of today even though in serious drama, film, and novel it has

come to accept, even expect, revelations of sexuality and perver-
sion beside which even the *ménage à trois* of *Design for Living*
seems stodgy. (Those in the audience who, like Mr. Whiting, are
no longer titillated by Coward's daring can respond to it as a sort
of nostalgia.) Thus, though it was a part of the 1920's challenging
of all conventional values, Coward's amorality is no less conventional than his praise of hearth and country in his more serious
plays; the only difference may be that, while the general theater
audience expects the writer to approach domestic bliss and patriotic enthusiasm with, at the very least, his tongue in cheek, they
accept anti-Puritanism at its own valuation.

Coward's comedies profit, in fact, from the feeling many people
have that not to be broadminded about morality—at least theoret-
ically, at least as a member of the audience at a "smart" play—is
to be excluded from truly civilized society. Eric Bentley is accurate in choosing *Fumed Oak* as an example of a farce in which the
audience's aggressions are given a direct yet socially approved
outlet,[10] but slapping one's mother-in-law, which Henry Gow
does in that play, is far less typical of Coward's plays than discon-
certing and shocking the outsider. While this too may express the
audience's aggressions, it also continually underlines the idea that
being shocked is itself the surest mark of the outsider. Still, when
the end of the play is reached, marriage and romantic love are
little damaged; and both sophisticated broadmindedness and conventional morality are found to be compatible.

Again, this combination is nothing new in the history of comedy, even, perhaps, in the most sophisticated high comedy. Shakespeare's Beatrice and Benedick in *Much Ado About Nothing* point
the finger of scorn at all the conventions of romantic love, but
they are married at the end; and, despite their wit and clear-
sighted judgment, their love is ultimately not much different from
Hero's and Claudio's in the same play. Mirabell and Millamant in
Congreve's *The Way of the World* display the depths of their love
by arranging for a sensible marriage, repudiating both adultery
and marriage based on anything but the most profound mutuality
of feelings; Restoration comedy as a whole, for all its bawdry and
air of exploding forever the canons of stuffy respectability, actually disparages only the loveless marriage, the one built on greed
(either sexual or economic) or on convenience, and while recognizing sexual drives as inevitable, considers them largely comic.

Comedy in general, even farce, stresses the need for reasonable behavior, conventional behavior somewhat trimmed of its hypocrisies and inflexibilities, its basic values really untouched. This conventionality in large part is what is meant by contending that traditionally comedy deals with human foibles, mankind's curable ills, and is hardly the vehicle for proclaiming a truly new ethic.

And yet, such a conclusion does not completely satisfy. Are the differences between Coward and Congreve only a matter of degree and not of kind, and has time changed only the surface but left the heart of comedy unaltered? Like Congreve, Coward concludes his plays with romantic marriage; but there is little pressure of feeling and conviction leading to that conclusion. Often, the end is achieved by a plot trick—Victor and Sibyl's quarrel reuniting Amanda and Elyot in *Private Lives;* Gilda, Victor, and Leo bursting into hilarious laughter at Ernest's anger in *Design for Living;* Garry, in *Present Laughter,* moving to his wife's apartment because matters have become too complicated in his own—which rounds the play off symmetrically, but rarely signifies anything.

The characters suffer from the same lack of meaning. Coward's witty couples stand out from their backgrounds because they are cleverer in their insolence, more articulate in their harangues, and better at understating their sentimentality but who could take any of them (with the possible exception of Serena and Axel in *Quadrille*) as patterns of mature elegance as one can view Mirabell and Millamant, or Beatrice and Benedick? Most of Coward's comic heroes and heroines are amusing only as residents of that never-never land where one need never grow up and may remain late-adolescent Peter Pans.

II *The Entertainer*

Study of content, then, brings the reader up short. At his most serious, Coward can deal effectively with the "gentler emotions— pity, compassion, nostalgia, love, regret"; but Mr. Rattigan can hardly be right when he says that, these are "likely to inspire the most worthwhile and durable drama": "Anger rarely breeds understanding, and without understanding a play becomes too subjective to make good drama. Exciting, perhaps, at its immediate impact; but forgotten soon afterwards." [11] No doubt understanding is a necessity for the playwright, but surely the most durable drama has dealt with something more than "the gentler emotions." Other than *Still Life*, all of the plays which can be labeled "serious" in any way have already dated badly. Without penetrating deeply into the historical situations or the characters created, these plays are touching and evocative; but they are rarely and inadvertently meaningful. Even *Post-Mortem*, Coward's one *cri de coeur*, is a collection of once fashionable attitudes only sporadically relieved by the sound of a living voice.

Quite the opposite is true of the comedies; there the voice is always clear and individual. A crisp, cool voice, it sometimes lapses into superciliousness, occasionally warmed by sentiment; but most characteristically it is lightly amused yet faintly contemptuous. The speaker seems like Garry Essendine, of *Present Laughter*, to be perceptive about the weaknesses of others and sometimes even about his own; yet, in the main, he is committed to his own gratifications and self-dramatization. Although he is the epitome of the elegant philanderer, clear-eyed without being excessively cynical, he settles for marriage; but both the philandering and the domestic life are little more than conveniences of the moment. Although a certain amount of sexual freedom is taken for granted, the main attitude is that of "to each his own," a tolerant attitude, but hardly a very dynamic one.

The high farces—*Hay Fever, Blithe Spirit, Hands Across the Sea, Pomp and Circumstance*—have virtually no subject matter at all and will probably prove to be the most durable of all Coward's work. Coward is at his best when his imagination is freed to play at pure make believe. Then his talents, somewhat cramped or obscured in his other work, are revealed in full glory and the essential Coward emerges: the supreme entertainer.

"Entertainer" is a more precise term than "man of the theatre," another familiar label. The latter puts the stress on technical expertise, on skill in exploiting the resources of the theater. It applies beautifully to Coward, but it applies as well to Shakespeare or Molière or Ibsen; the term says nothing about the uses to which the skills are put. The entertainer, on the other hand, need not have a wide range of skills; what matters is the way in which he looks at himself, at his material and, most important, at his audience. The entertainer exists not simply in the theater but in the spotlight. He presents, not an idea or even a mood, but simply himself for the audience's enjoyment; and the audience delights in this pleasure, in its awareness that all the cleverness and charm and glamor are for it. The spectators are not eavesdroppers on the artist's dialogue with himself, nor does he address them out of some need or desire to communicate, to explain or to convince; instead, they hardly wonder whether there is a man behind the personality.

Coward frequently expresses his exasperation with those who believe his true nature to be the same as that of the puppets he has created and played on the stage. But, his is in large part the misunderstanding; the audience has not so much confused the off-stage man with the on-stage character as paid him the compliment of preferring the far more vivid and individual persona he created. The audience has assumed that, as in the case of the magician and the clown, the man without his make-up and his props is simply too ordinary, too drab, too much like themselves at their dullest to be admitted to consciousness. The audience has recognized that the craftsman has always served the entertainer, and has paid its tribute to the former by applauding the latter.

The entertainer's job is to make time pass pleasantly, enjoyably, while making the audience forget about the time that is passing, to remove the present moment from the flux of time and erase, for a moment, both past and future. The purest entertainment is the perfect escapism, and Coward's high farces are his closest equivalent to the magician's suspension of gravity and logic. His aptest title is *Present Laughter,* and the chief device on his coat of arms should be a circle; for not only do almost all his plays end by returning to their beginnings, but their circularity, even when the play covers a good deal of time, is a denial of organic development and change and decay and time itself. The surest sign that Coward is really the craftsman that he wants the audience to recognize is the vividness and variety he has given to this view and the thoroughness with which he has confounded all those who predicted that—without his presence as performer, and as soon as theatrical fashions shifted a bit—even the best plays would simply evaporate. Yet there they are on the printed page, as brittle, as shallow, as mindless as ever; but they are still sealed within an envelope of special stage air, still breathing—still, astonishingly, alive.

Notes and References

Chapter One

1. Most of the material in this chapter is drawn from Noel Coward's first volume of autobiography, *Present Indicative* (Garden City, New York, 1937), and from the supplementary material, mostly names and dates, provided by Raymond Mander and Joe Mitchenson, *Theatrical Companion to Coward* (London, 1957). Only quotations of significant length are footnoted.

2. Coward, *Present Indicative*, p. 3.

3. Patrick Braybrooke, *The Amazing Mr. Noel Coward* (London, 1933).

4. Coward, *Present Indicative*, p. 44.

5. *Ibid.*, p. 73.

6. Robert Graves and Alan Hodge, *The Long Week-End* (London, 1940), p. 144.

7. John G. Rogers, "Noel Coward on Noel Coward," *New York* magazine, New York *Herald Tribune*, December 8, 1963, p. 35.

8. Bernard Shaw, "Beerbohm Tree," *Selected Prose* (New York, 1952), p. 552.

9. C. Haddon Chambers, *Passers-By* (New York, 1914), pp. 14–15.

10. Graves and Hodge, p. 127.

11. *Ibid.*, p. 147.

12. Noel Coward, "The Truth About Us Moderns," *Theatre World,* V (March, 1927), p. 13.

13. Coward, *Present Indicative*, p. 65.

14. *Ibid.*, p. 113.

15. John Montgomery, *The Twenties: An Informal Social History* (New York, 1957), p. 211.

16. J. C. Trewin, *Dramatists of Today* (London, 1953), p. 151.

Chapter Two

1. Coward, *Present Indicative*, p. 97.

2. Noel Coward, introduction to *The Noel Coward Song Book* (New York, 1953), p. 9.

3. *Ibid.*, pp. 11–12.
4. *Ibid.*, p. 71.

Chapter Three

1. See, for example, the cover of *Short Stories, Short Plays and Songs by Noel Coward* (New York, 1955).
2. Coward, *Present Indicative*, p. 187.
3. *Ibid.*, p. 194.
4. Noel Coward, introduction to *Play Parade* (Garden City, New York, 1933), p. x.
5. Noel Coward, introduction to *Play Parade*, Vol. II (London, 1950), pp. viii–x.
6. Review of *Easy Virtue*, New York *Times*, December 8, 1925.
7. James Agate, review of *Easy Virtue*, London *Sunday Times*, June 13, 1926.
8. Coward, *Present Indicative*, pp. 270–71.
9. St. John Ervine, review of *Sirocco*, London *Observer*, November 27, 1927.
10. Coward, *Present Indicative*, pp. 334–35.
11. *Ibid.*, p. 340.
12. *Ibid.*, p. 341.
13. *Ibid.*, p. 351.
14. Noel Coward, *Future Indefinite* (Garden City, New York, 1954), pp. 326–27.
15. Terence Rattigan, "Noel Coward," *Theatrical Companion to Coward*, p. 4.
16. Ivor Brown, review of "The Astonished Heart," London *Observer*, January 12, 1936.
17. Noel Coward, foreword to *Peace in Our Time* (Garden City, New York, 1948), pp. 13–14.
18. *Ibid.*, pp. 15–16.
19. Rattigan, p. 3.
20. G. B. Stern, quoted in Braybrooke, as being from a "recent magazine article," p. 162.

Chapter Four

1. John Gassner, *A Treasury of the Theatre: From Henrik Ibsen to Eugene Ionesco* (New York, 1961), p. 731.
2. Coward, *Present Indicative*, p. 166.
3. *Ibid.*, p. 211.
4. E. W. B., review of *Home Chat*, *Westminster Gazette*, October 26, 1927.
5. Ivor Brown, review of *Private Lives*, *Week-end Review*, October 4, 1930.

6. Coward, introduction to *Play Parade*, pp. xvi–xvii.

7. John Howard Lawson, *Theory and Technique of Playwriting* (New York, 1960), p. 152.

8. *Ibid.*, p. 153.

9. *Ibid.*, p. 152.

10. J. C. Trewin, review of *Relative Values, John O'London's Weekly*, December 14, 1951.

11. Geoffrey Tarran, review of *Quadrille, Morning Advertiser*, September 13, 1952.

12. Brown, review of *Private Lives*.

13. W. Somerset Maugham, introduction to Noel Coward, *Bitter-Sweet and Other Plays* (Garden City, New York, 1929), p. vi.

Chapter Five

1. Coward, *Future Indefinite*, p. 178.

Chapter Six

1. Frank Swinnerton, *The Georgian Scene* (New York, 1934), p. 435.

2. *Ibid.*, p. 449.

3. *Ibid.*, pp. 450–51.

4. *Ibid.*, p. 436.

5. John Raymond, "Play, Orchestra, Play!" *New Statesman*, LVI (October 25, 1958), p. 563.

6. Trewin, *Dramatists of Today*, p. 157.

7. *Ibid.*, pp. 151–52.

8. John Whiting, "Coward Cruising," *The London Magazine*, II (August, 1962), p. 66.

9. Quoted in Swinnerton, pp. 448–49.

10. Eric Bentley, "The Psychology of Farce," *Let's Get a Divorce and Other Plays* (New York, 1958), p. 12.

11. Rattigan, p. 4.

Selected Bibliography

Most of Noel Coward's plays have been published in many forms, usually as individual titles at first, then in collections of two or three, often in anthologies with plays by other authors and almost always in separate acting editions. In addition, most have been published in England and America at different times and in different formats, and some have had no American publication at all. The following is a selected list of collections and individual titles which provide the best texts in the most readily available form. Duplications are included where different collections or editions provide supplementary material not easily available elsewhere.

PRIMARY SOURCES

1. Plays

After the Ball. London: William Chappell, 1954. Lyrics and separate songs only.

Bitter-Sweet and Other Plays. New York: Doubleday, Doran and Co., Inc., 1932. Contains: Introduction by W. Somerset Maugham, *Bitter-Sweet, Easy Virtue, Hay Fever.*

Collected Sketches and Lyrics. New York: Doubleday, Doran and Co., Inc., 1932. Contains an assortment of materials from revues and musical plays, some available only in this collection.

Curtain Calls. New York: Doubleday, Doran and Co., Inc., 1940. Contains: *Tonight at 8:30, Conversation Piece, Easy Virtue, Point Valaine, This Was a Man.*

Look after Lulu! London: William Heinemann Ltd., 1959.

Nude with Violin. New York: Doubleday and Co., Inc., 1958.

Peace in Our Time. New York: Doubleday and Co., Inc., 1948. Contains a foreword not available elsewhere.

Play Parade: all volumes have introductory material by Coward.

    Vol. I. London: William Heinemann Ltd., 1934. (Published in America by Doubleday, Doran and Co., Inc., 1933, as *Play Parade;* volumes II–V, below, have never been published in America.) Contains: *Design for Living, Cavalcade, Private Lives, Bitter Sweet, Post-Mortem, The Vortex, Hay Fever.*

Vol. II. London: William Heinemann Ltd., 1950. Second edition. Contains: *This Year of Grace!, Words and Music, Operette, Conversation Piece, Fallen Angels, Easy Virtue.*

Vol. III. London: William Heinemann Ltd., 1950. Contains: *The Queen Was in the Parlour, I'll Leave It to You, The Young Idea, Sirocco, The Rat Trap, This Was a Man, Home Chat, The Marquise.*

Vol. IV. London: William Heinemann Ltd., 1954. Contains: *Tonight at 8:30, Present Laughter, This Happy Breed.*

Vol. V. London: William Heinemann Ltd., 1958. Contains: *Pacific 1860, Peace in Our Time, Relative Values, Quadrille, Blithe Spirit.*

Vol. VI. London: William Heinemann Ltd., 1962. Contains: *South Sea Bubble, Nude with Violin, Waiting in the Wings, Ace of Clubs, Point Valaine.*

South Sea Bubble. London: William Heinemann Ltd., 1956.

Suite in Three Keys. New York: Doubleday and Co., Inc., 1967. Contains: *A Song at Twilight, Shadows of the Evening, Come into the Garden Maud.*

The Plays of Noel Coward. New York: Doubleday, Doran and Co., Inc., 1928. (*Published in England as Three Plays with a Preface.*) Contains: preface, *Home Chat, Sirocco, This Was a Man.*

Three Plays. London: Ernest Benn, 1925. Contains: "Author's Reply to His Critics," *The Rat Trap, The Vortex, Fallen Angels.*

Waiting in the Wings. New York: Doubleday and Co., Inc., 1960.

2. Non-dramatic works

Australia Visited. London: William Heinemann Ltd., 1941. (Radio addresses)

Bon Voyage. New York: Doubleday and Co., Inc., 1968. (Short stories)

Chelsea Buns. London: Hutchinson and Co., 1925. (Satire)

The Collected Short Stories. London: William Heinemann Ltd., 1963.

"Echo of Laughter," *McCalls,* XCIII (February, 1966), 98–99. (Short story)

Future Indefinite. New York: Doubleday, Doran and Co., Inc., 1954. (Autobiography)

"Lie in the Dark and Listen," *Atlantic Monthly,* LCXXII (October, 1943), 98. (Poem)

"Lines to an American Officer," *The Saturday Review of Literature,* XXVI (October 16, 1943), 63. (Poem)

The Lyrics of Noel Coward. London: William Heinemann Ltd., 1965.

Middle East Diary. New York: Doubleday, Doran and Co., Inc., 1944. (Journal)

Pomp and Circumstance. New York: Doubleday and Co., Inc., 1960. (Novel)

Present Indicative. New York: Doubleday, Doran and Co., Inc., 1937. (Autobiography)

Pretty Polly and Other Stories. New York: Doubleday and Co., Inc., 1965.

Spangled Unicorn. New York: Doubleday, Doran and Co., Inc., 1933. (Satire)

Star Quality. New York: Doubleday and Co., Inc., 1951. (Short stories)

Terribly Intimate Portraits. New York: Boni and Liveright, 1922. (Satire)

"The Truth About Us Moderns," *Theatre World,* V (March, 1927), 13. (Essay)

To Step Aside. New York: Doubleday, Doran and Co., Inc., 1939. (Short stories)

SECONDARY SOURCES

Reviews of individual works, which constitute the bulk of comment on Coward's writing, are not included; a representative selection is available in *Theatrical Companion to Coward.*

Beerbohm, Max. *Heroes and Heroines of Bitter Sweet.* London: Leadlay, Ltd., 1931. A collection of splendid caricatures of Coward and of the performers in his operette.

Braybrooke, Patrick. *The Amazing Mr. Noel Coward.* London: Denis Archer, 1933. Written early in Coward's career, when each season brought new and startling evidence of his versatility and productiveness, this study is most useful in providing a picture of the almost idolatrous regard in which Coward was held by many in the early 1930's. Otherwise, the book is effusive and, to judge by the many discrepancies between it and Coward's own autobiographies, not very reliable.

Brown, John Mason. "English Laughter—Past and Present," *The Saturday Review of Literature,* XXIX (November 23, 1946), 24–28. Brief, rather obvious discussion of Wilde, Maugham, and Coward as social historians.

Ervine, St. John. "The Plays of Mr. Noel Coward," *Queen's Quarterly,* XLIII (Spring, 1935), 1–21. An excellent survey of Coward's work up to 1935, discussing the playwright as representative of the flippant yet despairing post-war generation, at once a Bright Young Man and "an embittered Puritan," but finally concluding that his characters are at best only "infant atheists," and that the substance of the plays is very thin.

Furnas, J. C. "The Art of Noel Coward," *Fortnightly Review*, CXXXIV (December, 1933), 709–16. Mainly a tribute to Coward's versatility, but with regret that his moral vision has not grown along with his technical virtuosity.

Greacen, Robert. *The Art of Noel Coward*. Aldington, Kent: The Hand and Flower Press, 1953. Despite its appearance between hard covers, this is only an essay, offering a sensible but sketchy overview of Coward's work.

Macdonnell, A. G. "The Plays of Noel Coward," *The Living Age*, XCI (January, 1932), 439–46. Sees most of Coward's work before *Private Lives* and *Post-Mortem* as a series of false starts, but looks ahead to Coward's development as a serious playwright.

Mander, Raymond, and Joe Mitchenson. *Theatrical Companion to Coward*. London: Rockliff, 1957. Absolutely indispensable, this volume provides full information on casts, dates of production, reviews, biographical background, bibliography, discography, and a great deal more. The introduction, "Noel Coward—an Appreciation of His Work in the Theatre," by Rattigan, is excellent.

"Noel Coward," *Saturday Review*, LCV (January 28, 1933), 92. Twin essays, "I Like Him Because" by Alpha and "I Dislike Him Because" by Omega, which wittily compress most of the critical issues.

Raymond, John. "Play, Orchestra, Play!" *New Statesman*, LVI (October 25, 1958), 563–64. The publication of *Play Parade*, Vol. V, is the occasion for a swift survey of Coward's work, particularly valuable for a perceptive discussion of Coward's mastery of "verbal triviality."

Rogers, John G. "Noel Coward on Noel Coward," *New York* magazine, New York *Herald Tribune*, December 8, 1963, p. 35. A recent interview, typical of the many published, this one revealing Coward as a warm optimist.

Snider, Rose. *Satire in the Comedies of Congreve, Sheridan, Wilde and Coward*. Orono: University of Maine Press, 1937. An examination of the satirical elements in *The Vortex, Hay Fever, Easy Virtue, Private Lives, Design for Living* and *Point Valaine*, concluding that Coward's comedy represents "a reversion to the freedom of the Restoration."

Swinnerton, Frank. "Post-War Pessimism," *The Georgian Scene*. New York: Farrar and Rinehart, 1934, pp. 433–59. A discussion of Coward along with Richard Aldington, Aldous Huxley, and Wyndham Lewis as representatives of 1920's despair, a point of view that seems more relevant to the others than to Coward.

Titterton, W. R. "Noel Coward," *Theatre World*, VII (December, 1927), 24. Probably the earliest attempt to do more than comment on an individual production or merely repeat gossip; concludes that Coward is "among the prophets," sounding the "note of protest."

Trewin, J. C. "Tap-Tap," *Dramatists of Today*. London: Staples Press, 1953, 151–61. Concise discussion of the main features of Coward's work.

Whiting, John. "Coward Cruising," *The London Magazine*, II (August, 1962), 64–66. Argues convincingly that Coward's awareness of the "mob at the gates" has betrayed him into raising his voice, although his true talent lies in an aristocratic, aloof, unassertive precision.

Woodbridge, Homer E. "Noel Coward," *The South Atlantic Quarterly*, XXXVII (July, 1938), 239–51. A general résumé of Coward's work through 1937, with primary concern for the serious plays; soundly predicts that "he will never write better plays than he has written."

Index